NON-CHRISTIAN RELIGIOUS SYSTEMS.

CHRISTIANITY

AND

BUDDHISM:

A Comparison and a Contrast.

BEING THE DONNELLAN LECTURES FOR THE YEAR 1889-90.
Preached in the Chapel of Trinity College, Dublin.

BY

T. STERLING BERRY, D.D.,

Rector of Birr, Diocese of Killaloe.

PUBLISHED UNDER THE DIRECTION OF THE TRACT COMMITTEE.

LONDON:
SOCIETY FOR PROMOTING CHRISTIAN KNOWLEDGE,
NORTHUMBERLAND AVENUE, W.C.; 43, QUEEN VICTORIA STREET, E.C.;
BRIGHTON: 135, NORTH STREET.
NEW YORK: E. & J. B. YOUNG & CO.

CONTENTS.

CONTENTS.

Metaphysical Buddhism—theory as to cause of Rebirth
—Rebirth and Moral Responsibility—Future Punishment—path of Deliverance—the Arahats—Nirvâna—
Max Müller's change of view—double sense of the word
Nirvâna—testimony of the Sacred Books—testimony of
the system as a whole—parallel suggested by Childers—
the Buddhist and the Christian Hope -   - pp. 71—93.

LECTURE V.

Buddhism a system rather than a Religion—the Ten Commandments—Order of Lay Disciples—Admission to the
Order—Life of the Bhikkhus—substitute for prayer—
Buddhist apatheia—classification of sins—beauty of
moral precepts—its defects—sorrow a false starting-
point—calculation of consequences—motives and rewards—Buddhist conception of human life—Christian
conception of life   -   -   -   - pp. 94—113.

LECTURE VI.

The story of Barlaam and Joasaph—Seydel's theory as to
the influence of Buddhism on Christianity—true view of
the Parallelisms—external and internal evidence—Rhys
Davids' theory—absence of Parallelisms—the Resurrection the keynote of Christianity—Oldenburg on the
Logia—place of Miracles in both systems—the Christian
and Buddhist Canon—our conception of Christ's claim—
Christianity and Buddhism in contrast   - pp. 114—135.

CHRISTIANITY & BUDDHISM:

A Comparison and a Contrast.

———•♦•———

LECTURE I.

St. John i. 9.—"The true Light which lighteth every man that cometh into the world."

In studying a religion different from that acknowledged amongst ourselves there are two dangers that have to be avoided. Some persons who have been in the habit of regarding all other religions as absolutely false—as partaking only of darkness, and in no sense of light, and finding when they begin to study them that their conceptions have been wrong, run at once into an opposite extreme; they use language in reference to the doctrines of these religions, and the Sacred Books in which the doctrines are enshrined, that is both exaggerated and misleading. So far from regarding their own religion as alone possessing light and truth, they now proclaim other religions to be as true as, or even more true than, that which they had been brought up to believe. For those who become enamoured of another religion become often strangely unjust

towards their own—they not only under-estimate
its worth, but they positively misrepresent its
teaching.

On the other hand there are some who fail in an
opposite direction : they fail to see beauty, light
or good in any but their own creed; they lack the
power of sympathy which is needful in order to
come in touch with those who are differently constituted and differently circumstanced.   Hence
they apply false standards of comparison and
adopt untrue conclusions.

Both these tendencies are illustrated in the case
of those who have written on Buddhism. By
some Buddhism and its Sacred Books are exalted
above Christianity and the Bible : to read their
words one would suppose that in Buddhism was
to be found unclouded light and spotless perfection ; and that in the Books of that religion there
was contained a store of wisdom, an exalted
morality, a poetic beauty unparalleled in the
records of any other creed.

In the general preface to his edition of " The
Sacred Books of the East," Prof. Max Müller has
called attention to this danger : " Readers who have
been led to believe that the Vedas of the ancient
Brahmans, the Avesta of the Zoroastrians, the
Tripitaka of the Buddhists, the Kings of Confucius, or the Koran of Mohammed are books full
of primeval wisdom and religious enthusiasm, or
at least of sound and simple moral teaching, will be
disappointed on consulting these volumes. Looking
at many of the books that have been lately published

on the religions of the Ancient World, I do not wonder that such a belief should have been raised; but I have long felt that it was high time to dispel such illusions, and to place the study of the ancient religions of the world on a more real and sound, on a more truly historical, basis." In a subsequent part of the preface he adds, " I confess it has been for many years a problem to me, aye, and to a great extent is so still, how the Sacred Books of the East should, by the side of so much that is fresh, natural, simple, beautiful and true, contain so much that is not only unmeaning, artificial and silly, but even hideous and repellent."[1]

Just in proportion as the worth of the Sacred Books of other religions is over-estimated, so is the Bible under-estimated and misrepresented. For example, Alabaster, the author of " The Wheel of the Law," thus expresses his reason for abandoning faith in the Scriptures and in the truth of Christianity : " Belief that we are ruled by an unjust law or by an unjust God, capable of having reserved His special love for a peculiar people, or of visiting on children the sins of their fathers, is too horrible."[2] If the writer of these words had studied the Bible with anything like the same care that he has given to Buddhist books he could scarcely have failed to recognize that if the Israelites were placed in a position of special privilege there was also special responsibility resting upon them,[3] and that the

---

[1] *Sacred Books of the East.* Vol. I., pp. ix. and xii.
[2] *The Wheel of the Law,* Preface xviii.
[3] Amos iii. 2 ; Rom. ii 17—29.

Divine Purpose in setting them thus apart was not
only to keep the light of truth shining amongst
men, but also in order that the nation might
become the medium of blessing to all humanity.[1]
As to the sins of fathers being visited on children,
those who deny the law not only resist the conclusions of science but the testimony of facts,
which all can observe for themselves. What the
Bible does is to balance the law of heredity with
the complementary law of personal responsibility.[2]

But whereas there are some who over-appreciate
Buddhism and Buddhist books, others err in an
opposite direction. One of the leading authorities
on Buddhism is the Rev. Spence Hardy, for many
years a Wesleyan missionary in Ceylon. His
" Eastern Monachism " and " Manual of Buddhism" are replete with information and bear evidence
of patient study and careful research, but his estimate of the Sacred Books betrays a mistaken
standpoint. "The priests of India," he writes,
" are encumbered by weapons that may be wrested
from their hands and used to their own destruction.
When it is clearly proved to them that their
venerated records contain absurdities and contra-
dictions, they must of necessity conclude that their
origin cannot have been Divine; and the foundation
of the systems being thus shaken, the whole mass
must speedily fall, leaving only the unsightly ruin
as a monument of man's folly, when he endeavours
to form a religion from the feculence of his own

---

[1] Genesis xii. 3; xviii. 19 (R.V.); Exod. xix. 6.
[2] Ezekiel xviii.

corrupt heart, or the fancies of his own perverted imagination."[1] It would not be hard to estimate the result of the work of a missionary who should adopt this line of thought.

I have said so much by way of introduction in order to clear the ground for the definition of what I hold to be the true method of regarding such a system as Buddhism.

As believers in Christianity we are firmly convinced that in our religion we have the mind and will of God revealed to us; that He who said " I am the Light of the World "[2] declared to man the nature and the requirements of God as none other could. Being both the representation and the manifestation of God—the effulgence of His Glory and the very Image of His substance[3]—He taught with a fulness and an authority that no other Divine Messenger could equal or even approach. At the same time be it never forgotten that God reveals Himself in many ways. As God of the whole earth He did not prove Himself forgetful of the nations that had strayed away from truth and knowledge. It would seem very hard to rid the minds of men of the old Jewish idea that God was only a national Deity—national at least in this sense, that He reserved all His favours for one nation and all His judgments for the rest of humanity. And yet one of the charter texts of Christianity assures us that " God so loved the

---

[1] *Eastern Monachism*, p. 166. [2] St. John viii. 12; ix. 5.
[3] Heb. i. 3 (R.V.).

world."[1] St. Peter, addressing for the first time a
Gentile audience, declared the new revelation
made to him that " God is no respecter of persons,
but in every nation he that feareth Him and
worketh righteousness is acceptable to Him."[2] St.
Paul, at Lystra, proclaimed that at no time had
God left Himself without witness amongst the
nations of the earth[3]; and at Athens he boldly
asserted that the universal purpose of God had
been that all men " should seek God, if haply they
might feel after Him and find Him, though He is
not far from each one of us."[4] And he does not
hesitate to quote the words in which Kleanthes
and Aratus had called the human race the offspring
of Zeus, as expressing the Catholic truth that all
men are sons of God.   We need not then think it
strange that in the Epistle to the Romans, where
St. Paul describes the hideous vices of heathen
nations, he should at the same time emphasize the
fact that they were partakers of Divine Light and
Divine Revelation.   The works of God in nature,
and the voice of God in conscience, so witness to
Him, the Apostle says, that they leave those without excuse who deny His Being or mistake His
requirements.   And that these revelations did not
altogether fail is manifest, as he adds that " nations
that have not the law do by nature the things of
the law, and these having no law are a law unto
themselves, in that they show the work of the law
written in their heart, their conscience bearing
witness therewith."[5]

[1] St. John iii. 16.   [2] Acts x. 34, 35.   [3] Acts xiv. 17.
[4] Acts xvii. 26—28.   [5] Rom. i. 18—20; ii. 14—16.

I do not think that it is possible to study with a fair and unprejudiced mind either the life of the great founder of Buddhism, or some of the books which his followers regard as their authoritative rule of faith, without feeling what a forcible illustration is here furnished of the truth of St. Paul's words.

Moreover, in the Prologue to St. John's Gospel, where Christian dogma is so marvellously expressed, the great fact of the Incarnation is founded on the relationship of Christ to the whole world as both its Creator and its Illuminator. " All things were made by Him, and without Him was not anything made that hath been made." . . . " There was the true Light, even the Light that lighteth every man, coming into the world."[1] So far then from feeling any difficulty when we find truth and beauty in Buddhist teaching, rather should we recognize therein a proof of the universality both of the Fatherhood of God and of the diffusion of that Divine Light which, though in varying degrees of brightness, does shine in some measure upon all the sons of men.

Buddhism stands in somewhat of the same relation to the old religion of India as Christianity does to Judaism, or in some respects more exactly as Protestantism does to Romanism. It represents in part a revolt and a reformation, in part also a process of growth and development. To understand the system it is therefore necessary

[1] St. John i. 3, 9.

to know something of what preceded it, and of the nature of the efforts which the early Hindu thinkers made to seek God if haply they might feel after Him and find Him.

India shared in the great tide of Āryan immigration, by which Europe and Persia were also affected. From the high table lands of Central Asia, near the source of the Oxus, the stream of population began to flow. Entering India by the mountain passes of its north-western frontier, the Āryan immigrants drove down before them the Turanian tribes who had colonized the country at a still earlier date. Establishing themselves first in the district of the Panjāb, they gradually spread down the valley of the Ganges, until they had occupied all Central India.

A good deal of the subsequent religious history of India turns upon the circumstances of this migration. The Indo-Āryan tribes came from an elevated and bracing district, where they had lived a hard but healthy life. The whole conditions of existence were altered in their new home. Subject to the influence of a relaxing and enervating climate, exposed to the burning heat of the sun, but surrounded by districts so fertile that but little toil was needed in order to supply themselves with food, together with the change of climate, the people themselves underwent a gradual but radical change.

For climate and surroundings affect the religious conceptions of men. Religion has its objective side, for it has to do with eternal truth and Divine realities; but religion has also its subjective aspect, since it is an answer to the wants and aspirations of the human heart.

Even in the same country and under the same conditions the disposition and temperament of people differ very largely. Much more is this true in the case of two races, living in different countries and subject to conditions and circumstances that vary as widely as possible. At root the words of the Psalmist are true of every human being, " My soul is athirst for God "; but the conditions of existence will largely govern both the mode in which the need will manifest itself to the individual heart, and the form in which the need will find expression.

Under healthy conditions the different elements in human nature are simultaneously developed: the inner and outer life are kept in equipoise— thought and emotion, action and energy go hand in hand—they mutually affect and control each other. But when this adjustment is disturbed, and one part of human nature is inordinately developed, the result invariably is an unhealthy product.

When the early Hymns of the Rig-Veda are compared with the later compositions included in it, and still more with the development of religious thought in India during the centuries that followed its compilation, we can see a signal illustration of this truth. The earlier Hymns, many of which were composed prior to the migration of the Āryans to India, are fresh, natural and simple ; the outcome of essentially healthy minds :

man was then looking out of himself, above himself; vaguely, but with a certain childlike simplicity, trusting and praying where it seemed to him that what his soul desired was likeliest to be found.[1] But after the migration to India a change gradually crept in: outer life was neglected: thought and reflection dominated over the activities of the bodily powers: the enervating and relaxing environment turned man's attention inordinately upon himself, and the result was altered conceptions of God, of the world, and of the life and destiny of man.

Various steps or stages have been noted in the history of religious thought at this period in India.[2] But it seems to me that, underlying the different and apparently contradictory forms which the dominant beliefs of the people assumed from time to time, there was a process of evolution which resulted in Pantheism as the recognised creed of Indian philosophy. The germs of Pantheism can be traced even in the later Hymns of the Rig-Veda.[3]

[1] Comp. Max Müller, *Lectures on the Science of Religion*, p. 93; and *Origin of Religion*, p. 228.

[2] Max Müller, *Origin of Religion*, Lecture vi.

[3] Comp. Barth, *Les Religions de l'Inde*, p. 7: "Voici maintenant, dans ses traits principaux, la religion qui nous est transmise dans les Hymnes. La nature entière est divine. Tout ce qui impressionne par sa grandeur, ou est supposé capable de nuire ou d'être utile, peut devenir un objet direct d'adoration. Les montagnes, les fleuves, les sources, les arbres, les plantes sont invoqués comme autant de puissances. Les animaux qui entourent l'homme, le cheval qui le traîne au combat, la vache qui le nourrit, le chien qui garde sa demeure, l'oiseau dont le cri lui révèle l'avenir, ceux, en plus grand nombre, qui menacent son existence, reçoivent

The history, however, of thought differs from
history that concerns external action in this
respect, that periods of transition are, as a rule,
less clearly marked, and that varying and even
opposite influences work simultaneously to a far
greater extent. For some time in India it would
have been impossible to foretell whether Poly-
theism, Monotheism, or Pantheism would prove
the dominant belief of the nation. Men who felt
within them yearnings after God were seeking for
the Great Spirit which they believed was somewhere to be found. At times and to some minds
it seemed as if many powers were at work, each
needing to be invoked and propitiated. To others
this conception was so unsatisfactory that they
preferred to believe that the One Supreme Power
manifested itself in many forms. Others went a
step further, and saw the Great Spirit everywhere :
within them, around them, above them. One of the
latest in date of the Hymns of the Rig-Veda thus
expresses this conception of the Great Spirit—

> " He is himself this very universe,
> He is whatever is, has been, and shall be,
> He is the lord of immortality."

For a time, however, this Pantheistic idea seemed
to pass into the background : there ensued a
period in which Ritualism became the predominant

un culte d'hommages ou de déprécations. Dans l'appareil
qui sert aux sacrifices, quelques pièces sont plus que des
objets consacrés, ce sont des divinités ; et le char de guerre,
les armes offensives et défensives, la charrue, le sillon qui
vient d'être tracé, sont l'objet non seulement de bénédictions,
mais de prières. Dès le berceau, l'Inde est foncièrement
pantheiste."

characteristic of the Hindu religion : the epoch of
sacrifice, marked by the supremacy of the Brāhmans, who arrogated to themselves a position and
an importance unsurpassed in the history of
Sacerdotalism.   Religion and sacrifice became for
the time being convertible terms : the blood of
victims was for ever flowing, and, together with
the sacrifices, there was elaborated a complicated
ritual that gave to the priestly office its importance
and unmeasured influence.   The Brāhmans were
regarded as the visible representatives of the Great
Spirit, the mediators between Heaven and earth.
Invested in popular belief with supernatural powers,
regarded as having in their hands the destiny of
man, capable of making the powers above his friend
or foe—entrusted with the entire charge of the
education of the young—free from all state control
and acknowledging no earthly ruler—it is impossible to measure the extent of the influence
which the Brāhmans exercised, or to realize the
estimation in which they were held.   Nevertheless, they escaped some of the dangers into
which, at other periods in the history of the world,
men have fallen who have been accorded a somewhat similar position.   For although gifts and
offerings were ceaselessly flowing in to them from
the willing hands of those who sought their aid,
yet those Brāhmans were held in highest esteem
who lived throughout, as many of them did, lives
of self-denying poverty, and who had their wants
supplied by begging their bread.

I have said that during all this period it would

seem as if the Pantheistic idea had been thrust
aside into obscurity, yet in reality such was not
the case. It is not without reason that we speak
of " waves of thought," for if the onward progress
of any great movement be watched, there will
always be found times in which it will seem to fall
back like the receding wave, but only to gather
strength for the next advance that is certain
soon to follow. So it was in India, for directly
after the Ritualistic era, Pantheism reasserted
itself with far greater power, and for the time
being won the victory over all rival forms of
thought.

Different influences combined to bring about
this result. The people grew weary of the never-
ceasing round of sacrifices, of the tedious and
meaningless ritual ; they felt that there was something unreal and unsatisfactory in making religion
consist in ordinance and ceremony, and they failed
to find in such service any rest or any true answer
to the needs of the human heart. Men began,
moreover, to argue on Pantheistic lines concerning
the unreasonableness of sacrifice : that if the
Divine Spirit be universally diffused, so that
nothing but it exists, a propitiatory sacrifice becomes at once a contradiction and an absurdity.

The Brāhmans themselves had no small share
in this movement : they had become practically
Pantheists, and their teaching of religion turned
into philosophical speculation, as they reasoned
concerning the Ātman, the spirit or soul of the
universe. This is the period of thought repre-

B

sented by the Upanishads—philosophical treatises,
the leading idea of which: is the uselessness of
sacrifice and ritual, and the paramount importance
of self-culture—the attainment of that self-know-
ledge which consists in the recognition of the true
self of each individual as a detached part of the all-
pervading Spirit, and which leads to its reunion
or reabsorption into that Spirit as its ultimate
goal.

In spite of the wearying repetitions, and what
appears to our minds the unmeaning phraseology so often to be found in these treatises, there
is nevertheless an interest in marking the efforts
by which the deepest thinkers in India at that
remote period of time strove to give expression to
their conceptions concerning God and the human
soul. The following extracts are taken from one
of the most ancient of the Upanishads; it will be
noticed that the word Brahman is used for the
world-Spirit, the nature of which it is sought to
explain: "The Brahman . . . . is the same as
the ether which is around us, and the ether which
is around us is the same as the ether which is
within us, and the ether which is within us, that is
the ether within the heart, that ether in the
heart (as Brahman) is omnipresent and unchanging.
He who knows this obtains omnipresent and unchangeable happiness" (*K*handôgya-Upanishad,
iii. Pra., 12 Kh., 7-9). "All this is Brahman.
Let a man meditate on that (visible world) as beginning, ending and breathing in it (the Brahman).
Now man is a creature of will. According to

what his will is in this world, so will he be when
he has departed this life. Let him, therefore,
have this will and belief: The intelligent, whose
body is spirit, whose form is light, whose thoughts
are true, whose nature is like ether (omnipresent
and invisible) from whom all works, all desires,
all sweet odours and tastes proceed; he who em-
braces all this, who never speaks and is never
surprised, He is my self within my heart, smaller
than a corn of rice, smaller than a corn of barley,
smaller than a mustard seed, smaller than a canary
seed, or the kernel of a canary seed. He also is
myself within the heart, greater than the earth
greater than the sky, greater than heaven, greater
than all these worlds. . . . . He, my self within
my heart, is that Brahman. When I have departed from hence I shall obtain him (that self)"
(*Kh.*-Up., iii. Pra., 14 Kh.). In the following
dialogue an effort is made to illustrate the same
thought : " Place this salt in water, and then wait
on me in the morning." The son did as he was
commanded. The father said to him, " Bring me
the salt which you placed in the water last night.'
The son, having looked for it, found it not, for, of
course, it was melted. The father said, " Taste it
from the surface of the water. How is it ? " The
son replied, " It is salt." " Taste it from the
middle and the bottom. How is it ? " " It is
salt." The father said, " Throw it away and then
wait on me." He did so ; but salt exists for ever.
Then the father said, " Here also in this body you
do not perceive the True, my son ; but there

indeed it is. That which is the subtile essence, in it all that exists has its self. It is the True. It is the Self and thou, O Svetaketu, art it." (*Kh*-Up. vi. 14.)

It must be noted, however, that there is a difference between this primitive Hindu Pantheism and what we understand by the term. The Hindu philosophers supposed that there existed one impersonal Spirit, of whom alone existence could rightly be predicated; a Spirit without consciousness, but which, through the operation of causes that act independently of its control, becomes conscious and personal, and manifests itself under different illusory forms, which cannot truly be said to have a real existence. To Ignorance and Illusion are due the severance of the self in man from the Self of the universe. So long as ignorance of the Self, its nature, and its origin lasts, this severance must continue. To overcome Ignorance and Illusion is man's highest aim, for thereby reabsorption into the great Spirit is secured to him ; and there in unconscious existence will be an eternal end to care and toil.

Three practical consequences followed from this conception. First, an intensely pessimistic view of human life. All things in the world were regarded as subject to the laws of impermanence and change. The higher the language that was used concerning the Ātman, the greater was felt to be the distance that separated the world and human life from all that was believed concerning it. It was described as " the self, free from sin, free from old age, from death and grief, from hunger and thirst, which desires nothing but what it ought to desire, and imagines nothing but what it ought to imagine.'' (*Kh.*-Up. viii. 1, 5). " As the sun, the eye of the universe, remains far off and unaffected by all sickness that meets the (human) eye, so also the one, the Ātman, who dwells in all creatures, dwells afar and untouched by the sorrows of the world."[1]

The perfection of that existence in which nothing was known of sickness and suffering, of decay and death, gave an intense prominence to the darker aspect of human life. The only refuge from its tedium and disquietude was believed to be the deep sleep, in which personal consciousness was for the time lost. Then during such sleep the self of the individual was supposed to return to the true Self. " Learn from me," so we read, " the true nature of sleep. When a man sleeps here, then he becomes united with the true, he is gone to his own (Self)." (*Kh.*-Up. viii. 6, 3.)

Closely allied with this pessimistic view or human life was the Hindu doctrine concerning the destiny of man. The remorseless tyranny of death was ever before the eye, intensified by the belief in transmigration, which involved the yielding by the individual of his body again and again to the dread power, whose sting, to the Hindu mind,

[1] Quoted by Oldenburg, *Buddha*, p. 43. He adds; "Here occurs for the first time the expression, 'Sorrow of the world' (Weltschmerz)."

was a fearful reality. Just as in the case of the Pantheistic idea, so here also the germ of the transmigration dogma can be traced back to the hymns of the Rig-Veda. There we find the idea that when death claims the body, the soul departs to dwell in the waters or the plants.[1] It is, however, only rarely and incidentally that the thought occurs during that period. But in the Brâhmanas, the text-books of Ritualistic Hinduism, transmigration is brought more prominently forward. In order to emphasize the paramount necessity for sacrifice, it was taught that at first the gods themselves were mortal, and that they continued so until they had overcome Death by sacrifice. When they had thus freed themselves, they made with Death this compact, that in order that it might still possess some power, no man should attain immortality without first presenting to it his body, and that those who neglected the prescribed sacrifices should die times without number.[2]

[1] Comp. Barth, *Les Religions de l'Inde*, p. 18: "On s'imaginait encore que l'individu venant à se dissoudre et à retourner aux éléments, son âme allait habiter les eaux, les plantes (Rig-Vêda, x. 58 ; 16, 3). Cette dernière conception, où il y a déjà comme une première ébauche de la theorie de la métempsychose, ne se trouve qu'exceptionnellement dans les hymnes du Rig-Vêda."

[2] Sir Monier Williams has thus translated the passage from the Satapatha-Brāmaṇa in which the compact is mentioned—

" The gods lived constantly in fear of Death—-
The mighty Ender—so with toilsome rites
They worshipped and repeated sacrifices
Till they became immortal. Then the Ender
Said to the gods, ' As ye have made yourselves
Imperishable, so will men endeavour

When, however, thought was concentrated on the Ātman, then as a necessary consequence the doctrine of transmigration occupied a foremost place in the speculations of Hindu philosophers. The selfs or souls of men, separated as they were from the True, could not but return again and again to the world so long as the severance lasted.

In the earlier stage of the belief sacrifice was regarded as the only method of deliverance; but with the discredit into which ritual fell as philosophy dominated, a new agency had to be sought by means of which the endlessly-recurring series of births and deaths might be brought to an end. In the discovery of the Self this deliverance was now supposed to consist. "As here on earth people follow as they are commanded, and depend on the object they are attached to, be it a country or a piece of land, and as here on earth, whatever has been acquired by exertion perishes, so perishes whatever is acquired for the next world by sacrifices and other good actions performed on earth. Those who depart from hence without having discovered the Self and those true desires, for them there is no freedom in all the worlds. But those who depart

To free themselves from me; what portion then
Shall I possess in man?' The gods replied,
'Henceforth no being shall become immortal
In his own body; this his mortal frame
Shalt thou still seize; this shall remain thy own,
This shall become perpetually thy food.
And even he who through religious acts
Henceforth attains to immortality
Shall first present his body, Death, to thee.'"

Brāhmanism and Hindūism, p. 24.

from hence after having discovered the Self and those true desires, for them there is freedom in all the worlds." (*Kh.*-Up., viii. 1, 5, 6).

To affect reunion with the Ātman thus became the highest quest. But since all action belongs to the sphere of the impermanent, there was nothing which man could in any proper sense *do*, in order to effect this consummation. Moreover, the very essence of action, according to Hindu philosophy, was that it bore fruit : of everything that man does he must reap the consequences : this was one of the fundamental conceptions upon which the doctrine of transmigration rested.

But, whereas there was nothing which a man might do, there was a great deal which he might *renounce*, and from which he might and ought to free himself, hence as a practical consequence followed Asceticism and the formation of monastic orders as securing the safest mode of life: "knowing him, the Ātman, Brahmans relinquish the desire for posterity, the desire for possessions, the desire for worldly prosperity, and go forth as mendicants."[1] He who has attained that supreme knowledge, the knowledge of the Self—the True, what remains on earth for him that he should prize or cling to it ? Far better to sever every possible tie, to quench the flame of desire, and to dwell in that actionless, passionless existence which approaches the dreamless contemplation wherein on earth the human soul comes nearest its eternal rest.

[1] Oldenburg, *Buddha*, p. 32.

It is impossible to look upon this picture of human life and faith and destiny without realizing something of its intense sadness. To the Brāhman who carried out his creed with conscientious exactness there was not left in life one element of light and brightness. The morbid development of thought, the outcome in part of his surroundings and still more of his non-natural mode of life, produced in him the gloomiest conceptions both of the present and of the future; for when the spirit of man can content itself with an unconscious, impersonal existence as its final goal, it has as much lost its health and vigour, as the body that would set sleep and rest before energy and activity.

And yet the intense earnestness of these men cannot fail to claim our admiration: their toilsome, patient searching after truth—their longing desire to rise above the material and transient to the spiritual and eternal—their devotion and whole-hearted effort for what they regarded as the noblest end of life and being—these characteristics have in them lessons for ourselves.

And surely we may trace, even in this strange development of human thought, part of that Divine discipline by which this race of men was being tutored and trained for higher life and fuller revelation. Nor need we doubt but that the Eternal Father who created them, who "determined their appointed seasons and the bounds of their habitation,"[1] so that they might feel after Him

[1] Acts xvii. 26 (R.V.).

and find Him, saw in their creed and in their philosophy something more than grotesque mistakes and irrational conceptions. *We* do not blame those who in the dim twilight suppose shadow to be form, and who mistake lifeless objects for living creatures. *We* do not find fault with little children for their strange questions and still stranger guesses in the days when knowledge begins to dawn upon their infant minds. And He, who seeth not as man seeth—who looks beneath the external and visible for the hidden motive and the secret aspiration, beheld, we may be sure of it, in this Hindu nation, amongst priests, philosophers, and people, many an earnest heart, whose deepest cry, like that of Job, was, " Oh ! that I knew where I might find Him," [1] and who, judging them according to that which they had, not according to that which they had not, accepted their desires, and pardoned their mistakes—made them partakers in the blessings of the Advent of our Lord Jesus Christ, and vouchsafed unto them what they groped after all their life long—the vision of light and truth in His eternal Presence in the Heaven above.

---

[1] Job xxiii. 3.

LECTURE II.

ST. LUKE xix. 26.—" Unto every one which hath shall be given."

IT has been necessary to trace the development of religious thought in the early history of Hindūism in order to be able to understand the relationship which Buddhism holds to the beliefs and conceptions previously existing in the nation in which it arose. There is not very much that is absolutely new in Buddhism : it is rather a fresh departure on, to a large extent, the old lines. Most, if not all, of its technical terms—some of its leading dogmas, had their established position in the accepted creed, and it is by understanding the previous significations given both to these words and doctrines that we can best grasp how their import was altered in the new movement which we have now to study.

The religions that have gained the greatest hold upon the human race—that have secured the largest number of adherents, and that have lasted for the longest period—have had personal founders. One whom we regard as unique in His Person, His Office and His Teaching is so inseparably connected with our religion that Christianity without Christ involves a contradiction in terms. Vyāsa, the reputed compiler

of the Vedas, and Zoroaster, the supposed founder
of the religion of the Parsīs, are personages too
mythical to found any argument upon their connection with the creeds of those who hold them
in reverence. But within the range of reliable
facts Confucius, Buddha and Mohammed are men
who stand out prominently in the annals of bygone
days as leaders of thought who have left a lasting
impress upon the religious history of the world.

It is sometimes hard to determine whether the
personal character of a great man, or the accident
of his birth at a particular time, has more to say
to his pre-eminence. But in the case of the
founder of Buddhism, this difficulty does not
apply. It was a time of varied thought in India
—in many directions, and by different methods
men were seeking to solve the enigmas of human
life and destiny. Dissatisfied with previous efforts
they were looking for a surer method of deliverance from toil and sorrow. These circumstances
prepared the way for the introduction of a new
creed. But, nevertheless, a contrast between
Brāhmanism and Buddhism leads to the conclusion that the success of the latter movement
was mainly due to the personal character and
history of its founder. Others possibly might
have thought out the system; but behind the
system there was the man. From those amongst
whom he lived, who beheld what manner of man
he was, he won the tribute of admiration; his
influence was founded on the estimation in which
he was held. And ever since, those who have

known his life, so far as it is possible to know it, have felt that he was a hero more worthy of the name than many to whom it has been accorded— a preacher of righteousness according to the light given to him—a consistent follower as well as teacher of the laws of purity, self-sacrifice and truth.

The life of its founder forms, therefore, a necessary part of the study of Buddhism. But at the outset we are met by the difficulty that there is nothing in the Buddhist Canon which corresponds to our Gospels. Legend has prevailed over history; extravagant myths and absurd miracles have proved more acceptable to the Eastern mind than simple statements of actual facts. And yet it is of primary importance to endeavour to separate truth from fiction, and to put together what may be reasonably regarded as reliable history in contrast with Buddha's legendary life. Many people who indulge in Buddhist conversation have contented themselves with the perusal of Sir Edwin Arnold's "Light of Asia," which, although a charming poem, is as reliable for the true life of the Buddha as would be a history of our Lord that was compiled indiscriminately from the New Testament, the Apocryphal Gospels, and the myths of the Middle Ages.

It may seem strange at first sight that the devoted disciples who survived the Buddha did not compose a record of his life that should preserve for succeeding generations the picture of one so loved and venerated.

It is only a partial explanation to say that the

Hindu mind was averse to history, and inclined to speculation. Beyond this there is a further reason which we can best appreciate by contrasting the earliest records of Christianity with those of Buddhism.

I shall have occasion to refer at length in a subsequent Lecture to the erroneous view maintained by Oldenburg that there is a parallelism—not a contrast, in the two cases—that the disciples of Christ cared at first to perpetuate His teaching alone, and at a later period thought for the first time of recording His life.[1] I can only here state that it was precisely the reverse of this that took place ; that it was Christ Himself, and the events of His life, that formed the subject both of the earliest teaching, and of the earliest literature in the Christian Church. The contrast in the two cases is based upon the different conception which the disciples of our Lord ha of their Master from that entertained of the Buddha by his followers.

It was the Person of Christ that impressed itself most deeply upon the first generation of Christians. His Mission even more than His Message, His deeds of love and mercy, His patient suffering, His self-sacrificing Death, above all His Resurrection from the dead, and His subsequent Ascension into Heaven, this was the subject matter of the proclamation first made by His followers to the world. On the other hand it was the *system* thought out by Buddha—the dis-

---

[1] Oldenburg, *Buddha*, pp. 79, 80 (English Translation). See Lecture vi., p. 127.

courses which he delivered, and his rules for the guidance of his disciples that appeared to them of paramount importance. They thought of him mainly as the Teacher, whereas the primary conception of the early Christians was of our Lord as the Saviour, who had accomplished, not merely taught, the salvation of the world.[1]

Hence it happens that the three main divisions of the Buddhist Canon are Discourses, Rules of Discipline, and Metaphysics; there is no life of the founder of the creed. It is then no easy matter to endeavour to distinguish between fact and legend; and it is not surprising that some have been disposed to make legend account for everything, or else to minimize the facts so as to leave the least possible residuum of reliable history. Sénart in his ingenious Essay on "The Legend of the Buddha," adopts this standpoint. He admits the actual existence of the founder of Buddhism, and, with a certain reservation, some few incidents in his life. But he believes that the old solar myths have been so largely incorporated into Buddhist legend that it is wholly impossible to feel certain as to any of the incidents of its founder's history. There is undoubtedly a strong element of truth in Sénart's reasoning; but where it seems to fail is that he makes legend displace fact; whereas it is far more reasonable to suppose that legend distorts and overlies fact. There is an essential

[1] See Acts ii. 22—35, iii. 13—21, x. 36—44, xiii. 23—39; 1 Cor. xv. 1—11.

difference between the two views.   According to
Sénart, facts are hopelessly lost, conjecture is the
sole foundation for reconstructing the life of the
Buddha. But according to the other view the facts
are there, obscured and perverted, it is true, but
capable of being recovered with a reasonable degree
of probability. Now, if not only the Gospels, but the
whole New Testament had been lost, and if we
had to reconstruct an historical record of our
Lord's life from the Apocryphal Gospels, and the
information that could be gleaned from early
Church writers, we should, nevertheless, feel that
He had a real existence, and that His Person and
history were of the first importance in moulding
the thoughts and beliefs of those who called themselves by His Name.   And there is this parallelism between Christianity and Buddhism, that the
centre of both systems is a Personal Founder.   Is
it, then, reasonable to suppose that the adoption
of existing myths so obliterated from the minds
of the early Buddhists the memory of their
teacher's life that no actual trace of his history
survives?   Surely it is far more probable that
by a gradual process, which the different existing
forms of the legend discloses, a superstructure
of legend was erected on a foundation of real
occurrences.

There are in the recognised Sacred Books
some scattered notices, and putting these together
and combining them with the historical element,
intermixed with later tradition, it is possible, I
believe, to give a reliable sketch of Buddha's life.

In the sixth century before Christ there lived among the *S*ākya tribe at Kapila-vastu a Rājah named Suddhodana. He had married the daughters of the Rājah of the Koliyans, a tribe that lived on the other side of the stream Kohāna, that formed the boundary between the two clans. For many years he was childless; but at length Māya, the elder of the two sisters, to his intense joy, bore him a son. The child was born as his mother was on a journey to her parents' home, and seven days after his birth she died, leaving the infant boy to be brought up by her sister. He was named Siddārtha Gautama. As to the name Gautama, the surname, as we should call it, there does not appear to be any doubt : the personal name " Siddārtha," which means, " He who has accomplished his purpose," may only represent a traditional title grounded on the circumstances of his life. The name *S*ākya-muni, that is " sage of the *S*akya tribe," is manifestly titular, as are also the other names by which he is described both in the Sacred Books and the legends. The circumstances of his birth of themselves led to his being surrounded in his early years with special watchfulness and care. Three residences were provided for him, adapted to the different seasons of the year. But of his early life and education very little can be definitely stated. Two facts alone appear trustworthy : his marriage to his cousin Yasōdharā,[1] and his triumph when, either before or

[1] She is only once apparently mentioned in the Pâli Pi*t*akas, and then not by name, viz., Mahâvagga I. 54, 2 (*S.B.E.*, Vol. xiii., p. 208).

C

after his marriage, it was objected against him by his wife's relatives that he neglected manly pursuits, for at a trial of skill he was proved to surpass all other competitors.

It was in his twenty-ninth year that the crisis of his life occurred. It is said that it was when the tidings were brought to him that his wife had borne him a son, that he felt that there had come a new tie to bind him to home and friends, and that at once, if ever, he must renounce all that he held dear, and enter upon a new era in his history.

We cannot willingly relegate to the region of myth the touching detail that when he desired to embrace the little infant ere he quitted his home, and found that the mother's arm was beneath its head, he refrained from fulfilling his purpose, lest he should rouse her from sleep, when her grief might disarm his resolution.

It must be noted, however, that the halo which tradition and poetry have set around what is generally termed " The Great Renunciation " is not by any means justified by the earliest comments on this event. In Col. Olcott's " Buddhist Catechism"—approved by the Principal of the Buddhist Priests' Training College, at Colombo, as being in agreement with the Canon of the Southern Buddhist Church, the following question and answer occur : Q. " Did any other man ever sacrifice so much for our sake ? " A. " Not one ; this is why Buddhists so love him, and why good Buddhists try to be like him."

Now set in contrast with such language as

this the statements of the ancient Buddhist Books: "Distressing is life at home, a state of impurity; freedom is in leaving home. While he reflected thus, he left his home."[1] What is here said about him is confirmed by the Discourses attributed to Gautama himself: " In him who has intercourse (with others) affections arise (and then), the pain which follows affection; considering the misery which originates in affection, let one wander alone like a rhinoceros. He who has compassion on his friends and confidential (companions), loses (his own) advantage, having a fettered mind; seeing this danger in friendship, let one wander alone like a rhinoceros. Just as a large bamboo tree (with its branches) entangled (in each other, such is) the care one has with children and wife; (but) like the shoot of a bamboo, not clinging (to anything), let one wander alone like a rhinoceros."[2]

If we try to estimate what prevailed with Gautama to renounce his home, even though we have to speculate as to his motives, it is possible to determine their probable nature. He is by no means the only man who found luxurious living, sensual gratification and perpetual pleasure-seeking incapable of satisfying the desires of the heart and productive rather of disgust and unrest. Possessed, as he must have been, of a nature exceptionally endowed with high and noble gifts,

[1] Quoted by Oldenburg. *Buddha,* p. 105.
[2] Khaggavisânasutta, 35--37 (*Sacred Books of the East,* Vol. x., p. 6).

a nature in which the spiritual element strongly predominated, it would have been strange indeed could he have contented himself with his original mode of life. It seems to me that we can trace an experience very similar to that through which Gautama passed in the opening chapters of the Book of Ecclesiastes, where the various efforts to obtain satisfaction all end with the same dismal refrain, " Vanity of vanities, all is vanity and a striving after the wind." If there be added to this the further fact that the ascetic life had already commended itself to the teachers of highest repute in India, we can well understand how one to whom the spiritual was of infinitely greater worth than the natural—who had learned that " a man's life consisteth not in the abundance of the things which he possesseth,"[1] should be impelled by the very force of his convictions and of his yearning aspirations after truth and rest, to abandon a life which failed to satisfy, and to enter a new path which seemed to promise the fulfilment of his heart's desires. That it cost him a struggle we need not doubt ; nor that during the painful years of disappointed anticipation he must many a time have been tempted to relinquish the quest and to resume the luxurious, easy life of former days. For it was not until he had made trial of the recognized methods of deliverance, that Gautama struck out a new path for himself. It is said that he resorted in the first instance to two prominent Hindu philosophers (Alāra and Udraka), the representa-

[1] St. Luke xii. 15.

tives in all probability of two leading schools of thought at that time. Finding their methods unsatisfactory, he next tried the plan of extreme asceticism and self-mortification. In the woods of Uruvelā he lived for six years, subjecting himself to the severest penances. Five hermits who lived near watched with wonder his rigid austerities; he partook scarcely of any food, and his strength gradually failed until one day he fell to the ground as dead.

Then ensued another crisis in his history. He slowly recovered from the state of prostration to which his recent mode of life had brought him, but he now freely partook of food, for he had come to the conclusion that he had been treading a wrong path, which would never lead to the fulfilment of his desires. His five companions at once deserted him. It seemed to them that he had abandoned the struggle and acknowledged himself vanquished. And hence in absolute solitude he was left to think out some more excellent way. Seated under a tree—known thenceforward as the Bo tree, or tree of knowledge, he remained for long absorbed in thought. At length the light broke in upon him. It appeared to him that he had solved the great problem, and that he had discovered the true path of deliverance. He had become the Buddha, the enlightened one, for the mists of error and ignorance had melted before the light of new heart-satisfying knowledge. For some time he remained in quiet, enjoying the bliss of emancipation. What came next is thus expressed

in the Sacred Books, "Then in the mind of the
Blessed One, who was alone and had retired into
solitude, the following thought arose: 'I have
penetrated the doctrine which is profound, difficult
to perceive and to understand, which brings
quietude of heart, which is exalted, which is un-
unattainable by reasoning, abstruse, intelligible
(only) to the wise. This people on the other
hand, is given to desire, intent upon desire,
delighting in desire. . . . . Now if I proclaim the
doctrine and other men are not able to understand
my preaching, there would result but weariness
and annoyance to me.' "[1] Better counsels however
prevailed: a noble-hearted man who believed that
he had discovered the way of truth could not
forbear from revealing this knowledge to others.
Consequently he determined to become a teacher
of men, and he had now only to decide where his
work should begin. He bethought him of the two
philosophers to whom he had gone when he quitted
his home, but learning that they had died, he
determined to preach first to the five Ascetics who
had been his companions in the wood of Uruvelā.

They were convinced partly by Gautama's
altered appearance, partly by the force of his
words; and from these six men, Gautama and the
five Ascetics, the Buddhist Brotherhood had its
source. In a short time his followers numbered
sixty; they belonged, it is said, to the highest
families in the country; and these men were now
sent out by him to preach the new doctrine through

[1] Mahâvagga I. 5, 2 (*S. B.E.*, Vol. xiii., p. 84).

the land. It is interesting to learn the words in which he delivered their commission to them :— " The Blessed One said to the Bhikkhus: ' I am delivered, O Bhikkhus, from all fetters human and divine. You are also delivered from all fetters human and divine. Go ye now and wander for the gain of the many, for the welfare of the many, out of compassion for the world, for the good, for the gain and for the welfare of gods and men. Let not two of you go the same way. Preach the doctrine which is glorious in the beginning, in the middle, in the end, in the spirit and in the letter ; proclaim a consummate, perfect and pure life of holiness. There are beings whose mental eyes are covered by scarcely any dust, but if the doctrine is not preached to them, they cannot attain salvation. They will understand the doctrine.'" [1]

In the records of Gautama's ministry there are only fragmentary notices of his personal history. Information as to the different places in which he stayed is given solely as an introduction to a conversation or discourse ; here as elsewhere, the system obscures the man. Even as to his teaching there is much omitted that would be of interest to know. His public life lasted for about forty-five years. We cannot think that the system, such as it was taught by his followers after his death, presented itself in its entirety to his own mind from the first. We should like to be able to trace the course of thought, and to note how his

[1] Mahâvagga I. 11, 1 (S. B. E., Vol. xiii., p. 112).

conceptions of life became gradually moulded as time went on. But this is impossible, and there does not seem to be any prospect that by the accession of new material the missing details will ever be supplied. There is, moreover, very little to guide us as to the various arguments brought to bear by him against the teaching of his opponents. His recorded interviews with them have a wearisome sameness. To know how one was convinced is to know every case. The result is invariably the same. The disputant acknowledges himself vanquished, and begs to be admitted into the Brotherhood.

There are, however, some few facts that can be gleaned from the scattered historical notices that belong to this period of Gautama's life. Shortly after he sent out his sixty followers to preach, the band of men who subsequently formed the inner circle amongst his disciples adopted the new creed.

Sāriputra and Moggallāna, who were so speedily advanced to a position of prominence that the envy of the other members of the Brotherhood was for a time aroused against them; Ānanda, Gautama's cousin, to whom, of all his followers he was most deeply attached; Devadatta, another cousin, who became the leader of the great Buddhist schism; and Upāli, who had been a barber, but who rose to a position of leadership in the order—a signal illustration of Gautama's disregard of caste in matters that affected religion.[1]

---

[1] It is important, however, to notice that whereas Gautama opened the Order to members of every caste without making any distinction between them, nevertheless he by no means

Some time after the system had been established a new departure was taken by the formation of an association of female mendicants. It was not without reluctance and misgiving that Gautama consented to their admission into the order.[1] He seems to have fully shared Oriental prejudices in this respect, and to have foreseen that there were inevitable risks involved in making the concession. It was only after urgent entreaty, first from his aunt, who had brought him up from infancy, and subsequently, after he had refused to hearken to her request, from Ānanda, that an unwilling consent was extorted from him. And that, nevertheless, he felt he had acted unwisely, appears from what he is reported to have said to Ānanda, that the result of the admission of women would be that his law would only last five hundred years, whereas it would have continued for a thousand years in the world had they been excluded.[2]

The number of his adherents would seem to have increased rapidly. No weight can be given to the extravagant figures which Oriental fancy delights to mount up in order to embellish a narrative. But underlying these exaggerations there is the fact that his career was marked with almost unbroken success. The element of suffering or even

undervalued the advantages of belonging to a high caste. One of the rewards of virtue was rebirth as a Brâhman or a Kshatriya. *See* Childers, *Pali Dictionary*, s.v. *Samano ;* Burnouf, *Introduction*, pp. 173, 188 ; Barth, *Les Religions de l'Inde*, p. 75.

[1] See Appendix IV.

[2] Kullavagga x. 1, 6 (S. B. E., Vol. xx., p. 325).

of open opposition entered very slightly into his experience. There was a murmur of discontent in the district of Magadha at an early period in his teaching. The populace cried out against him, that he had come to destroy family life, by inducing the young to quit their homes and enter the order. When this was reported to Gautama, he replied, " This noise will not last long ; it will only last seven days. . . . . . If they revile you, O Bhikkhus, you should reply, ' It is by means of the true doctrine that the great heroes, the Tathâgatas lead men. Who will murmur at the wise, who lead men by the power of the truth?'"[1] The soft answer seems to have turned away wrath, for we hear nothing more of such discontent. Another trouble was of a more serious nature. Devadatta, Gautama's cousin, aspired to be the leader of the Brotherhood, and accordingly he suggested to Gautama that, as he was now advanced in years, he should retire in his favour. Upon his refusal, Devadatta conspired against him ; the conspiracy failed. And then Devadatta tried a more artful plan. He made five propositions to Gautama, which were designed to alter the constitution of the Brotherhood by giving it a more rigidly ascetic complexion. When Gautama declined to adopt the suggestions, Devadatta attempted, with for the time a certain measure of success, to create a dissension in the Order, and to induce some of the Mendicants to follow him. It is said, however, that those who

[1] Mahâvagga I., 24, 6 (S. B. E., Vol. xiii., p. 151).

joined in the secession speedily returned to their allegiance, and that Devadatta himself came to a woeful end.[1]

With these exceptions it does not appear that Gautama had much to bear as the direct result of his position. I have said that Buddhism stands to Brāhmanism in something of the same relationship that Protestantism does to Romanism, and yet the career of Gautama differed very essentially from that of Luther. There seems to have been a considerable amount of tolerance in India at that time. Different schools of philosophy existed side by side; the current of thought was flowing fast. There were few, if any, cherished convictions. Men on all sides were ready to welcome the propounder of a new system; it was an era of seekers after truth rather than of champions for established creeds. Add to this the fact that Gautama both adopted and adapted many previously existing terms and conceptions, and it becomes easy to understand how little direct opposition he had to meet.

His life was active, but peaceful. Eight months of the year he spent itinerating through the country, principally in the districts of Magadha and Kosala; for the four rainy months, from June to October, he remained in retreat with his followers, engaged in meditation and instruction. When he was on his journeys, wherever he came he was eagerly sought out. Kings and nobles contended for the honour of entertaining him.

[1] Kullavagga vii. 2—4 (S. B. E., Vol. xx., pp. 233—265).

Wealthy merchants presented him with parks. No gift was too precious to be bestowed on him. Yet he never accepted any gift as a personal offering; what was given was the property, not of an individual, but of the Order.

It is hard not to believe that there is a historical foundation for the narrative which describes Gautama's visit to his old home at Kapila-Vastu. His aged father was desirous of seeing him before he died; but when Gautama entered the town clad in the mendicant dress, and, in accordance with custom, went with his alms bowl from door to door, his father went out in indignation and reproached him with putting him to shame by seeking alms in his own city. He replied that he was but following the example of his predecessors, and, thereupon he preached the new doctrine to him, declaring that when a man had found a hidden treasure, it was his duty to present to his father the most precious jewel. Suddhodana made no reply, but led him to his house. There he met Yasōdharā, who, as she saw him, burst into tears and fell down and caught him by the feet. But as she remembered his changed position, she arose and stood apart in silence. When consent was given by Gautama to the admission of women into the Order, Yasōdharā was one of the first who was enrolled as a female mendicant.

It is said that upon the occasion of this visit of the Buddha to his home his son Rāhula was also taken into the Brotherhood. And surely there is a touch of nature in the story that relates that when the aged Suddhodana heard this, in his distress at being deprived of the grandchild who was the sole hope of his declining years, he came to Gautama and induced him to enact that thenceforward no young person should be admitted into the Order until his parents or guardians had given their consent.

The historical records, that almost cease for so large a part of the Buddha's ministry, resume with the narrative of his death. His words and deeds during the closing days of his life are recorded with a fulness and minuteness that reveal the hand of reverence and love. In "The Book of the Great Decease," each stage of his last journey, each conversation with his faithful followers is given in detail.

It is remarkable that we find here the only miracle which this portion of the Buddhist Canon ascribes to Gautama. And the context furnishes an interesting illustration of how the miraculous element entered into the traditions concerning him. We read, " The Blessed One went on to the river. And at that time the river Ganges was brimful and overflowing, and wishing to cross to the opposite bank, some began to seek for boats, some for rafts of wood, while some made rafts of basketwork. Then the Blessed One, as instantaneously as a strong man would stretch forth his arm, or draw it back again when he had stretched it forth, vanished from this side of the river, and stood on the further bank with the company of the brethren."

In immediate connexion with this narrative there follow the words, " And the Blessed One beheld the people looking for boats and rafts, and as he beheld them he brake forth at that time into this song—

> " ' They who cross the ocean drear,
>   Making a solid path across the pools,
>   While the vain world ties its basket rafts,
>   These are the wise, these are the saved indeed.' " [1]

Without applying to Buddhist miracles modes of argument to which we object when they are used against the miracles of the New Testament, it is evident in this case that the miracle was an afterthought, and that it arose out of a materialistic or realistic construction put upon the illustration that Gautama employed.

As his end drew near his exhortations to his followers became earnest and constant, and their desire to learn from him was equally strong. We are told that Ānanda, his constant companion, besought of him, ere his life closed, to leave instructions concerning the Order, " What then, Ānanda," he replied, " does the Order expect that of me ? I have preached the truth without making any distinction between exoteric and esoteric doctrine ; for, in respect of the truths, the Tathāgata has no such thing as the closed fist of a teacher who keeps some things back. Surely should there be anyone who harbours the thought, ' It is I who will lead the Brotherhood,' or ' The Order is dependent upon me,' it is he

[1] Mahâ-Parinibbâna-Sutta l., 33 (S. B. E., Vol. xi., 21).

who should lay down instructions in any matter
concerning the Order. Now, the Tathâgata harbours no such thoughts. Why, then, should he
leave instructions in any matter concerning the
Order? I, too, O Ânanda, am now grown old
and full of years, my journey is drawing to its
close. I have reached my sum of days. I am
turning eighty years of age. And just as a worn-
out cart can only with much additional care be
made to move along, so methinks the body of the
Tathâgata can only be kept going with much
additional care. . . . Therefore be ye lamps
unto yourselves. Be ye a refuge to yourselves.
Betake yourselves to no external refuge. Hold
fast to the truth as a lamp. Hold fast as a refuge
to the truth. Look not for refuge to any one
besides yourselves. [They who do this] it is they
who shall reach the very topmost height. But
they must be anxious to learn."[1]

" My age is now full ripe, my life draws to a close,
I leave you, I depart, relying on myself alone!
Be earnest then, O Brethren! holy, full of thought!
Be steadfast in resolve! keep watch o'er your own hearts!
Who wearies not but holds fast to this truth and law
Shall cross this sea of life, shall make an end of grief."[2]

I can come to no other conclusion than that in
this Book we stand to a very large extent on the
foundation of historic record. The discourses
which it contains have many touches of originality
and genuineness. And the fact that it relates

[1] Mahâ-Parinibbâna-Sutta l. 32—35 (*S. B. E.*, Vol. xi., p.
36—39).
[2] *M. P. S.* iii., 66 (*S. B. E.*, Vol. xi., p. 61).

that the immediate cause of Gautama's death was
that he partook too freely of dried boar's flesh is
so painfully unpoetical that it can scarcely be
regarded as an invention of later days.[1] There is
a considerable difference of opinion as to the date
of his death. In the Ceylon chronicles it was
stated to be B.C. 543, but that date is now known
to be erroneous. Max Müller gives B.C. 477 as the
probable year. Oldenberg says B.C. 430. Sir
Monier Williams, B.C. 420, and Prof. Rhys
Davids, B.C. 412, while Profs. Kern and
Westergaard bring down the date to B.C. 370.[2]

The general estimate of the Buddha and his
work must be deferred until we have studied the
system which formed the basis of his teaching.
And yet it would be impossible to close this sketch
of his history without noticing that it furnishes an
illustration of a truth repeatedly brought out in
the New Testament, that the attainments of the
human soul do not correspond with *à priori*
anticipations.

Our Lord found the strongest faith in the least
likely quarters. Of a soldier in the Roman army
He said, " I have not found so great faith, no, not
in Israel";[3] his conception of the power of Christ
to heal, even at a distance, by a word, put to

---

[1] *M. P. S.* iv., 17 (*S. B. E.* xi., 71).

[2] The uncertainty arises from the fact that prior to
*K*andragupta, who reigned B.C. 315 to 291, all the dates of
Indian history are theoretical and tentative.

[3] St. Matthew viii. 10.

shame the imperious impatience of the Jewish
nobleman, who cried, " Sir, come down, ere my
child die."[1] To a descendant of one of the old
tribes of Canaan, Christ said, " O woman, great is
thy faith."[2] And drawing a general conclusion
from such instances He taught, " Many shall
come from the east and from the west and shall
sit down with Abraham and Isaac and Jacob in
the kingdom of Heaven."[3] Can we then for a
moment doubt that one who lived this pure and
noble life, in which without hope of any reward he
gave himself to the service of his fellow-men,
when he might have lived in luxury and ease, shall
be numbered amongst those who shall come " from
the east " ?

For, so far as we can judge of it, the life of
Gautama was a pure, unselfish, devoted life. I
cannot coincide with the estimate of Saint-
Hilaire that " His life had not a stain in it."[4]
Our knowledge of his history should be largely
increased before we could be justified in passing
such a verdict.

But even with the imperfect materials in our

---

[1] St. John iv. 49.   [2] St. Matthew xv. 28.
[3] St. Matthew viii. 11.

[4] " Je n'hésite pas à ajouter que, sauf le Christ tout seul, il
n'est point, parmi les fondateurs de religion, de figure plus
pure, ni plus touchante que celle du Bouddha. Sa vie n'a
point de tache. Son constant heroisme égale sa conviction,
et si la théorie qu'il préconise est fausse, les exemples per-
sonels qu'il donne sont irréprochables. Il est le modèle
achevé de toutes les virtus qu'il prêche ; son abnégation, sa
charité, son inaltérable douceur ne se démentent point un seul
instant."—Saint-Hilaire, *Le Bouddha et sa Religion*, p. xxxiii.

D

possession, we can find very much to admire—a record that puts to shame the life of many whose light is far greater than was his.

We can only dimly speculate as to what further training schools of discipline may await such souls—but that there are such seems a legitimate inference alike from the universal law, " Unto every one that hath shall be given,"[1] and from that most blessed promise, " He that doeth truth cometh to the light, that his deeds may be made manifest, that they have been wrought in God."[2]

---

[1] St. Luke xix. 26.   [2] St. John iii. 21.

LECTURE III.

ST. JOHN vi., 67, 68.—" Then said Jesus unto the twelve, Will ye also go away ? Then Simon Peter answered Him, Lord, to whom shall we go ? Thou hast the words of eternal life."

IN the last Lecture I endeavoured to put together the events in the life of Gautama that can be re- garded as reasonably probable ; not, indeed, that they all stand on the same level of historic support. For some facts there is the evidence of the Sacred Books ; for others only the probability derived from the circumstance that they seem to form the basis of later legends, or else that they are not such as would tempt the fancy of an imaginative disciple in after days. And in some cases it must be left an open question whether what is associated with the story of the Buddha be fact or legend. The legen- dary element intruded itself at an early date : the actual records were too plain and simple to suit Oriental fancy ; the zeal and devotion of Buddhists found an outlet in inventing a life of their Master according to what they believed it ought to have been. There are many circumstances connected with the growth of Buddhist legends that are of interest to ourselves. When we are confronted with the statement that in the Gospel History, as it has been handed down to us, legend has pre- vailed over fact, it is important to be able to point to a case in which such a process actually occurred : for it is by a comparison of this kind that we can most plainly see how untenable the Mythical theory becomes as an explanation of the records of the New Testament.

Sénart, from the view he holds as to Buddhist legends, is specially interested in throwing back the date of the legends as far as possible. Believing that few, if any, traces of Gautama's real history survive, it becomes incumbent upon him to fix the introduction of the myths as near as he can to the period of his life. Yet even he admits that an interval of about one hundred and fifty or two hundred years must be allowed for the formation of the legendary life.[1] To establish a parallel in Christian records, our earliest Gospel should date between A.D. 180 and 230 ; in other words, nearly a century subsequent to the publication of the latest of the Gospels.

Moreover, in the case of Buddhism the process of legend-making continued for a considerable period. There exist at the present time different versions of Gautama's mythical life : it is by no means difficult to arrange them in order of date, for they exhibit a process of expansion and a growth in extravagance. Now if you compare different accounts of some transaction, and if you find you can arrange them in order at once of

[1] Sénart, *Essai sur la Legende du Bouddha* "Certes, cent cinquante ou deux cents ans suffiraient, et au delà, pour expliquer la constitution de sa légende, dans les conditions que fera ressortir cette étude." Introd., xxiii.

length and of wonder, you will naturally conclude
that the longest and most wonderful record is the
latest in date. This is just what is found in
Buddhist legends; the latest form of the story is
what is contained in the Lalita Vistara, a work
written partly in poetry and partly in prose, and
which was composed between six hundred and
one thousand years after Gautama's death.

Like some of the Apocryphal Gospels, it only professes to give the history of Gautama from his birth
to the beginning of his public life. But it differs
from the Apocryphal Gospels in this respect, that
they never took any real hold of the members
of the Christian Church. Their inferiority to the
Canonical Gospels was so great and so glaring
that they were by common consent relegated to a
well-merited obscurity. But the Lalita Vistara
attained a high degree of popularity ; it was translated into different languages, and it was treated as
Canonical and historic. It serves to illustrate
how differently minds are constituted. To us its
perusal is one long trial of patience ; the exaggerations are so absurd, the miracles so innumerable,
the details and repetitions so wearisome that one
is often tempted to give it up in disgust.

It includes, however, an ancient element. There
are some places in which all the versions of the
legendary life run on the same lines. I select one
of these partly because it is a case in which legend
has been generally regarded as history, and partly
because we can not only trace it down through the
different stages of the legends, but also we can trace

it back to its source, so that it serves as an illustration of how the mythical element entered into the beliefs concerning the story of the Buddha.

When Gautama's father was informed by the astrologers that if the infant boy remained in the palace he would become a king of kings, but that if he abandoned his home he would be a Buddha, he set himself, the legends say, to hide from the child all knowledge of the sorrow and misery of the world. He was not allowed to wander outside the precincts of the palaces provided as his residences, and those of his attendants who became sick were at once removed, and others substituted in their place. As Gautama grew up he began to fret against this restraint, and one day directed his charioteer to drive him outside the palace walls. When the Rājah was informed of what was about to take place, he gave a reluctant consent; but before permitting his son to see the outside world, he gave strict directions that everything offensive to the eye was to be removed from the road which his son was to pass over. None but the young and healthy were to show themselves, and the streets were to be adorned with all things beautiful. Every precaution proved vain. On successive occasions there appeared visions, first of old age, then of sickness, and then of death, before the eyes of the Prince. Each time he inquired in wonder of his charioteer what the visions meant; and learning that it was the common lot of humanity to grow infirm and old, and then to die, he became deeply dejected; and though his father, when he heard what was taking place, redoubled his efforts to distract the Prince's mind with pleasures and allurements of many kinds, he failed to find any enjoyment in what was provided for him.

A fourth vision appeared in the form of a dignified sage, who had renounced the world; and when he heard the interpretation of this vision, the idea seized his mind that he too would go forth from the palace and embrace the ascetic life.

When he returned to the palace that evening " women clad in beautiful array, skilful in the dance and song, brought their musical instruments, and ranging themselves in order, danced, and sang, and played delightfully. But Gautama took no pleasure in the spectacle, and fell asleep. And the women, saying, ' He for whose sake we were performing is gone to sleep, why should we play any longer,' laid aside the instruments they held and lay down to sleep. Shortly after Gautama awoke, and looking on them as they lay asleep, a profound disgust for all that was sensual took possession of him, and forthwith he left his home."[1] This incident in the legends furnishes, as I have said, an illustration of their growth. As we follow down the different versions of the story it grows longer and longer, until in the Lalita Vistara it takes up a considerable space owing to the multiplication of details.

[1] Rhys Davids' *Buddhist Birth Stories*, Nidānakathā, pp. 76—81; Beal's *Romantic Legend*, pp. 107—130; Foucaux, *Le Lalita Vistara*, Annales du Musée Guimet, Tome sixième, pp. 166—184.

But what is more important, we can trace the legend back to its source. In the Sacred Books we read that the sixth disciple who joined Gautama was Yāsa, a youth of noble birth. He is represented as possessing three palaces and being surrounded with luxury, but awaking one night and looking on the sleeping forms of his attendants, he became disgusted with the palace life, and took refuge with the Buddha.[1]

With some such incident as a foundation, and the repeated use of such illustrations as old age, sickness, and death in Gautama's teaching to set forth the impermanence of human existence and human delights, it is easy to understand how the legend arose, and how the incident became associated with Gautama's own story.

The spiritual conflict through which he passed beneath the sacred tree where he obtained enlightenment, furnishes another congenial theme for the legendists. Here again there was most probably a foundation in actual fact. In addition to the mental process through which he passed as he thought out his system, there was almost certainly something further. It is a psychological truism that every crisis in the spiritual history of a man is the outcome of a conflict. Life's fiercest conflicts are those that are fought out on the battlefield of the human heart. The greatest leaders of men have been those who have experienced the deadliest brunt of such inner struggles. And with one in whom the spiritual element was as strong as it was

[1] Mahavâgga I , 7, 1-3 (S. B. E., Vol. xiii., p. 102).

with Gautama, it would be contrary to all precedent if he was not scarred with the wounds of that soul warfare through which those must pass who are real and honest seekers after truth.

The legends introduce a personal antagonist, Māra, the prince of darkness, who is represented as dogging the footsteps of Gautama from the time he determined on quitting his home till his final victory was won. The history of the name is interesting, and not without its parallel. Māro originally meant " Death," or " killing." Then it came to signify a personal tempter, supposed to be one of the three celestial Archangels, and owing his exalted position to the fact that in a previous state of existence he exercised to a high degree the virtue of charity. He is nevertheless a wicked angel, and his pleasures are those of sense. He is represented as having three daughters, Concupiscence, Love, and Anger. Māra came also to have an impersonal meaning. It was used broadly for the evil principle, and the Archangel was then regarded as merely one of its manifestations.[1] Against Gautama Māra is said to have summoned all his array, so as to baffle him in his efforts and deprive him of his influence. It can readily be imagined what a fruitful field this would furnish for legend and miracle. Signs and portents are so accumulated that one can only pause and marvel at the fertility of the imagination that gave them birth.[2]

[1] Childers, *Pali Dictionary*, s. v. Māro.
[2] Foucaux, *Le Lalita Vistara*, pp. 257—287.

Closely allied with the legends—to some extent their source—are the Jātaka Tales or Buddhist Birth-stories, which are to this day the delight of the adherents of the system as they meet together to keep festival. One leading characteristic in Gautama's teaching was the large use that he made of illustration. Sometimes he chose a brief but striking simile, sometimes he spoke a parable or told a story. When he desired to enforce a lesson or convey a reproof, his usual method was to relate an anecdote, which purported to be an account of what had happened to himself and the other persons concerned in some previous state of existence. The underlying idea on which these narratives were founded was that a Buddha is not created all at once ; that he is rather the ultimate product of a long development. And that when he has become the Buddha he can look back on the various stages through which he has passed and call to mind the occurrences which took place in previous states of existence. It can readily be supposed that on such a theory an inventive mind could frame any number of tales and describe a very varied experience.

The following Birth-story possesses a special interest for us: " A woman carrying her child went to the future Buddha's tank to wash. And having first bathed the child, she put on her upper garment and descended into the water to bathe herself. Then a wicked fairy seeing the child, had a desire to eat it. And taking the form of a woman, she drew near and asked the mother if the child was hers; and when she was told that it was, she asked if she might nurse it. And this being allowed, she nursed it a little and then carried it off. But when the mother saw this she ran after her and cried out, ' Where are you taking my child to?' and caught hold of her. The wicked fairy boldly said, ' Where did you get the child from? It is mine.' And so quarrelling they passed the door of the future Buddha's judgment-hall. He heard the noise, sent for them, inquired into the matter, and asked them whether they would abide by his decision. And they agreed. Then he had a line drawn on the ground, and told the fairy to take hold of the child's arms and the mother to take hold of its legs, and said, ' The child shall be hers who drags him over the line.' But as soon as they pulled at him the mother, seeing how he suffered, grieved as if her heart would break. And letting him go, she stood there weeping. Then the future Buddha asked the by-standers, ' Whose hearts are tender to babes, those who have borne children or those who have not?' And they answered, ' O Sire, the hearts of mothers are tender.' Then he said, ' Whom think you is the mother—she who has the child, or she who has let him go?' And they answered, ' She who has let go is the mother.' Then he exposed the theft of the wicked fairy, and the mother of the child exclaimed, ' O my lord, O great physician! may thy life be long!' And she went away with her child clasped to her bosom."[1]

[1] Abbreviated from Rhys Davids' *Buddhist Birth Stories,* Vol. i., p. xiv.

The similarity of this story to the Judgment of
Solomon is so great that there is the temptation to
claim for them a common origin.   Prof. Rhys
Davids supposes that the Jews may have told the
story at Babylon during the Captivity, and that it
spread gradually through different Eastern countries.   He rejects the idea, which seems to me far
more probable, that it came to India through the
traders who plied their ships between India and
Palestine in Solomon's reign.   He argues that
diversity of language must have rendered any
verbal communications between the two countries
very meagre.[1]   But when it is remembered that
the ships must often have been detained for a considerable period either at Joppa or at Ophir, it does
not seem too much to suppose that enough of the
language was picked up to enable the story to be
told and understood.   And if Ophir be identified
with the Abhîra at the mouth of the Indus,[2] it is sufficiently near the districts where Buddhism had its
origin to allow of the story travelling thus far.   The
only other tenable explanation seems to be that the
same idea presented itself independently to two
minds.

Many of Æsop's fables can be traced back to
a Buddhist original.   In fact, rightly regarded,
these fables are only Western adaptations of old
stories brought to Europe from the East.

Some of the Birth-stories undoubtedly belong
to a very remote antiquity: it may with con-

[1] *Buddhist Birth Stories*, Vol. i., pp. xlv.—xlvii.
[2] Duncker, *History of Antiquities*, Vol. ii., pp. 188, 265.

fidence be affirmed that not a few of them
were spoken by Gautama himself. A collection,
however, of this kind is liable to additions;
any good story that was in circulation would
be included in it, and the historical settings,
prefixed to the tales, which purport to give the circumstances that led to their utterance, are, as a
rule, manifestly false.

In order to gain an idea of the power of
similitude which the early Buddhists possessed
we must turn to the Dhammapada, a work which
belongs to the Sutta Pitaka, and which is one
of the most beautiful of their Sacred Books.
The meaning of its title is, according to Max
Müller, either "Path of Virtue," or "Footsteps
of the Law."[1] It is a collection of verses, bearing
in form, and sometimes in phraseology, a striking
resemblance to the Book of Proverbs. In its present form it can only claim a secondary place in
regard to antiquity, for it undoubtedly is a compilation of gems of thought from different Sacred
Books. Brief sayings, striking from their form
or matter, are put under different headings; and in
this respect also it is like the Book of Proverbs,
which is far more composite in date and authorship
than is generally supposed. As to the authenticity
of the Dhammapada Max Müller says, " I cannot
see any reason why we should not treat the verses
of the Dhammapada, if not as the utterances of
Buddha, at least as what were believed by the

[1] *Sacred Books of the East*, Vol. x., p. xlvi.

members of the Council under Asoka in B.C. 242 to
have been the utterances of the founder of their
religion."[1]

The following extracts will illustrate the character
of the Book. I select some because of their parallelism with texts of Scripture: "Hatred does not
cease by hatred at any time—hatred ceases by
love; this is an old rule."[2] Compare "If thine
enemy hunger, feed him; if he thirst, give him
drink; for in so doing thou shalt heap coals of fire
upon his head. Be not overcome of evil, but overcome evil with good."[3] A subsequent verse in the
Buddhist Book is almost identical with the text I
have quoted, it says, "Let a man overcome anger
by love, let him overcome evil by good; let him
overcome the greedy by liberality, the liar by
truth."[4] The familiar saying in the Book of
Proverbs, "He that is slow to anger is greater
than the mighty; and he that ruleth his spirit than
he that taketh a city,"[5] finds its parallel in the
verse, "If a man conquer in battle a thousand
times thousand men, and if another conquer
himself he is the greatest of conquerors."[6] As the
Proverb assures us, "A soft answer turneth away
wrath, but grievous words stir up anger,[7] so the
Buddhist Book teaches, "Do not speak harshly to
anybody; those who are spoken to will answer
thee in the same way. Angry speech is painful,

[1] *Sacred Books of the East*, Vol. x., p. xxv.
[2] *Ib.*, Dhammapada, 5.
[3] Romans xii. 19—21, and Proverbs xxv. 21, 22.
[4] Dh., 223.   [5] Prov. xvi. 32.
[6] Dh., 103.   [7] Prov. xv. 1.

blows for blows will touch thee."[1] There are
parallelisms also with New Testament teaching. The verse, " The thoughtless man, even if
he can recite a large portion (of the law) but is not
a doer of it has no share in the priesthood, but is
like a cowherd counting the cows of others,"[2]
reminds us of the words of St. James, " Be ye
doers of the word and not hearers only, deceiving
your own selves."[3] The precept, " Not the
perversities of others, not their sins of commission or omission, but his own misdeeds and
negligences should a sage take notice of,"[4] recalls
our Lord's warning, " Why beholdest thou the
mote that is in thy brother's eye, but considerest not the beam that is in thine own eye."[5]
And as He taught, " Beware of false prophets
which come to you in sheep's clothing but
inwardly they are ravening wolves;"[6] and, " Ye
cleanse the outside of the cup and of the platter,
but your inward part is full of extortion and
wickedness,"[7] so the Buddhist Book says, " Many
men whose shoulders are covered by the yellow
gown are illconditioned and unrestrained, such evil-
doers by their evil deeds go to hell."[8] " What is
the use of platted hair, O fool ? what of the raiment
of goatskins ? within thee there is ravening, but
the outside thou makest clean."[9] There are more
parallels to our Scriptures in the Dhammapada than

[1] Dh., 133.   [2] Dh., 19.
[3] St. James i. 22.   [4] Dh., 50.
[5] St. Matthew vii. 3.   [6] St. Matthew vii. 15.
[7] St. Luke xi. 39.   [8] Dh., 307.
[9] Dh., 394.

I have found in the rest of the Buddhist Books; the selections I have given are only a few out of many similar instances.[1]

It may be well, however, to mention here what I shall have to refer to at greater length afterwards, that if the theory be maintained that these parallelisms necessitate the conclusion that the one religion has borrowed from the other, a strong case can be made out for the dependence of Buddhism on Judaism, for the similarities between its Sacred Books and the Old Testament Scriptures are both numerous and striking.

I add a few more extracts from the Dhammapada to illustrate the beauty and power of thought that some of these brief maxims contain. Its opening verse runs thus, " All that we are is the result of what we have thought : it is founded on our thoughts : it is made up of our thoughts. If a man speaks or acts with an evil thought, pain follows him, as the wheel follows the foot of the ox that draws the carriage."[2] Again we read, " Not to commit any sin, to do good, and to purify one's mind, this is the teaching of (all) the awakened."[3] " There is no fire like passion ; there is no losing throw like hatred ; there is no pain like the body ; there is no happiness higher than rest."[4] " As the impurity which springs from the iron when it springs from it destroys it : thus do a transgressor's own works lead him to the evil path."[5]

[1] See Appendix II.   [2] Dh. 1.   [3] Dh. 183.
[4] Dh. 202.   [5] Dh. 240.

In the frequent use of illustration we find a similarity between Gautama's method and the teaching of our Lord.

There is the similarity, and yet at the same time a wonderful contrast—a contrast not only in the subject matter, but in the form in which the illustrations are put. In Buddhist literature, stories, similes, and fables abound ; parables in the strict sense of the term are far less frequent. But classing together all that may be grouped under the common heading of illustrative teaching in Buddhism, and setting it side by side with the Parables and similitudes of our Lord, it is the contrast, not the parallelism, that strikes the mind. To emphasize the uniqueness of this aspect of the teaching of Christ—to show that His Parables are absolutely unexampled, and that they have therefore not only a spiritual but also an evidential value, I do not know of any course better than to compare them with these Buddhist illustrations, and thereby to observe the contrast. I do not think that this fact is generally recognised. On the contrary a far stronger parallelism is supposed to exist than the actual circumstances warrant. In turning, for example, to the table of contents in Rhys Davids' "Buddhism," we find, under chapter v., "Parable of the Mustard Seed" and "Parable of the Sower." This at once suggests a very remarkable likeness to the teaching of our Lord. But the titles are most misleading ; the former, that is, the "Parable of the Mustard Seed," is in no sense a parable ; and the latter, if it has

E

any claim to the name of parable, ought to be headed "The Parable," or as I should prefer to say, "The Illustration of the Plough." For it is said that on one occasion Gautama came with his almsbowl to where a wealthy landowner was distributing food to his workmen; when he saw him approach, he began to reproach him with his idle life, "I, O Samana, both plough and sow, and having ploughed and sown, I eat. Thou, also, shouldest plough and sow, and having ploughed and sown, thou shouldst eat." "I also, O Brâhmana, both plough and sow, and having ploughed and sown, I eat," so said Bhagavat. "Yet we do not see the yoke, or the plough, or the ploughshare, or the goad, or the oxen of the venerable Gotama." Bhagavat answered, "Faith is the seed, penance the rain, understanding my yoke and plough, modesty the pole of the plough, mind the tie, thoughtfulness my ploughshare and goad. I am guarded in respect of the body, I am guarded in respect of speech, temperate in food, I make truth cut away (weeds), tenderness is my deliverance, exertion is my beast of burden, carrying me to Nibbâna, he goes to the place where one does not grieve. So this ploughing is ploughed, it bears the fruit of immortality: having ploughed, this ploughing one is freed from all pain."[1]

The incident of the mustard seed is one of the most touching of all the Buddhist stories, but it will be seen at once that the heading, "The Parable of the Mustard Seed," suggests a wrong train of

[1] Sutta Nipāta, 75—79 (S.B.E., Vol. x., p. 12).

ideas. A young girl named Kisāgotamī had married the only son of a wealthy man. She had one child, but when the beautiful boy could run alone, he died. The young girl in her love for him carried the dead child clasped to her bosom, and went from house to house of her pitying friends asking them to give her medicine for it. But a Buddhist mendicant, thinking that she did not understand, said to her, " My good girl, I myself have no such medicine as you ask for, but I think I know of one who has." " O tell me who that is," said Kisāgotamī. " The Buddha can give you medicine for him," was the answer. She went to Gautama, and doing homage to him, said, "Lord and Master, do you know of any medicine that will be good for my child?" " Yes, I know of some," said the Teacher. Now it was the custom for patients or their friends to provide the herbs which the doctors required, so she asked what herbs he would want. " I want some mustard seed," he said. And when the poor girl eagerly promised to bring some of so common a drug, he added, " You must get it from some house where no son, or husband, or parent, or slave has died." " Very good," she said, and went to ask for it, still carrying her dead child with her. The people said, " Here is mustard seed, take it." But when she asked, " In my friend's house has any son died, or a husband, or a parent, or slave?" they answered, " Lady, what is this that you say? The living are few, but the dead are many." Then she went to other houses, but one said, "I have lost a son"; another, "We have lost our parents"; another, "I have lost my slave."

At last, not being able to find a single house where no one had died, her mind began to clear, and summoning up resolution, she left the dead body of her child in a forest, and returning to the Buddha, paid him homage. He said to her, "Have you the mustard seed?" "My lord," she replied, "I have not. The people tell me that the living are few, but the dead are many." Then he talked to her on that essential part of his system—the impermanency of all things, till her doubts were cleared away, and accepting her lot, she became a disciple.[1]

The story is touching and beautiful in its way. Not only, however, does the title that I have quoted suggest an unfounded parallelism, but the incident itself furnishes a striking illustration of the contrast between the system of Gautama and the Gospel of Christ. Sorrow is a factor, terribly real and terribly common in human experience. Go to those who are in sorrow—who have lost one dear to them—and say, "All men have sooner or later to die; trouble at some time visits every home. Death impartially knocks at the door of the poor man's garret and the palace of the rich; therefore you have no right to complain if you have to participate in that which is the common lot of all." Go with such words as these and you

[1] Rhys Davids' *Buddhism*, p. 133.

will bring but cold comfort to the troubled
heart. And yet this is all that Buddhism can
say; it is the lesson of the incident I have just
quoted.

But take with you another story, and the effect
will be very different: " And it came to pass the
day after that He went into a city called Nain, and
many of His disciples went with Him, and much
people. Now when He came nigh to the city,
behold there was a dead man carried out, the only
son of his mother, and she was a widow. And
when the Lord saw her, He had compassion on
her, and touched the bier, and they that bare
him stood still. And He said, 'Young man, I
say unto thee, Arise.' And he that was dead sat
up and began to speak, and He delivered him to
his mother."[1] The miracle belongs to the past,
but a similar record is made by our Lord the illustration of an eternal and universal truth, for He
said on His way to the grave of Lazarus, " I am
the Resurrection and the Life, he that believeth
in Me, though he were dead, yet shall he live; and
He that liveth and believeth in Me shall never
die."[2]

Gautama taught a system; but Christ preached
a Gospel. Those who listened to Him were
able to say in reply to His appeal, "Do ye
also wish to go away?" "Lord, to whom shall
we go? Thou hast the words of eternal life."[3] And
the greatest of His disciples was able to teach,

---

[1] St. Luke vii. 11—15.   [2] St. John xi. 25, 26.
[3] St. John vi. 68.

" Sorrow not as the rest which have no hope.   For if we believe that Jesus died and rose again, even so them also which sleep in Jesus will God bring with Him.   Wherefore comfort one another with these words."[1]

[1] Thess. iv. 13, 14, 18.

LECTURE IV.

1 St. John ii. 25.—"And this is the promise that He hath promised us, even eternal life."

I HAVE so far endeavoured to treat the life of the founder of Buddhism and the manner of his teaching apart from the system itself, not only because it requires separate consideration, but still more because it is impossible to do justice to it without a previous knowledge both of its originator and of the pre-existing conceptions incorporated into it. It is to a larger extent true that you must know Brāhmanism in order to understand Buddhism than that you must study the Old Testament to grasp the teaching of Christianity. In fact with us the New Testament throws more light upon the Jewish Scriptures than they do upon the Revelation of Christianity. The New Testament could stand alone and be understood to a large extent without the aid of an acquaintance with any antecedent Revelation. The Old Testament, on the other hand, is a sealed book if it is treated as final and complete in itself. But the links that unite Brāhmanism and Buddhism are so many and so strong that the two systems must be studied concurrently. Some have gone so far as to affirm that Gautama was throughout a consistent and devoted Hindu.

This, however, is to affirm more than facts warrant. While adopting some existing conceptions and adapting others, so as to make them harmonise with his system, Gautama rejected and ignored too many accepted dogmas to allow of his being regarded merely as the leader of a new school of thought within the pale of an established religion.

I have pointed out that three dominant beliefs lay at the root of Indian philosophy at this period, namely, Pessimism, Pantheism, and the doctrine of Transmigration. We have now to see what Buddhism has to say in reference to these matters.

From the first Gautama taught that his system was a mean between two extremes—of both of which he had had some experience. " There are," he said, " two extremes which the man who has given up the world ought not to follow: the habitual practice on the one hand of those things whose attraction depends upon the passions, and especially of sensuality: a low and pagan way (of seeking satisfaction), unworthy, unprofitable, fit only for the worldly minded, and the habitual practice, on the other hand, of asceticism (or self-mortification), which is painful, unworthy, and unprofitable." [1]

In common with other leaders of thought at that time, it was a method whereby inward rest and peace might be obtained, which Gautama sought, a rest and peace which, existing in some measure

[1] Dhamma-Kakka-Ppavattana-Sutta, 2 (*S.B.E.*, Vol. XI., p. 146); compare also Mahâvagga I., 6, 17 (*S.B.E.*, Vol. XIII., p. 94).

in the present, should find their full fruition at the
end of life. Hence, in describing the middle path
which he had discovered, he speaks of it as "that
path which opens the eyes and bestows understanding, which leads to peace of mind, to the
higher wisdom, to full enlightenment, to Nirvāna."[1]

The creed—if it may be so termed—in which
this middle path is formulated, is contained in the
Four Noble Truths that form the essence of
Buddhism. They are thus briefly summed up :
" Pain, the origin of pain, the destruction of pain,
and the eightfold holy way that leads to the quiet-
ing of pain."[2] It appears at once that the system
is based upon the pessimistic view of human
existence which characterized prevalent Hindu
philosophy. And this becomes even more evident
when we read the expansion of this brief summary
of the truths in the discourses attributed to the
Buddha. " Now this is the noble truth concerning suffering : Birth is suffering, old age is suffering, sickness is suffering, death is suffering, to be
united with the unloved is suffering, to be separated
from the loved is suffering, not to obtain what one
desires is suffering. In brief, the conditions of
individuality and their cause, the clinging to
material form, sensations, abstract ideas, mental
tendencies, and mental powers involve suffering."
The second truth concerns the origin of suffering :
" Verily it is that thirst (or craving), causing the
renewal of existence, accompanied by sensual
delight, seeking satisfaction, now here, now there

[1] *S.B.E.*, Vol. XI., p. 147.   [2] Dhammapada, 191.

—that is to say, the craving for the gratification of the passions, or the craving for (a future) life, or the craving for success (in this present life)." The third truth describes the extinction of suffering : " Verily it is the destruction, in which no passion remains, of this very thirst; the laying aside of, the getting rid of, the being free from, the harbouring no longer of this thirst." And the fourth truth teaches the path which leads to the destruction of sorrow : " Verily it is this noble eightfold path, that is to say, 'right views, right aspirations, right speech, right conduct, right livelihood, right effort, right mindfulness, and right contemplation.' "[1]

There are certain fundamental conceptions which lie at the root of these truths. The first I have already referred to, namely, the inseparable connection between existence and sorrow. In drearier words even than the Book of Ecclesiastes contains, the life of man is described. And there is superadded the other belief, to which the Preacher was a stranger, that existence has a tendency perpetually to reproduce itself. There are, Buddha taught, chains and fetters, which bind each individual to existence, which bring him back to the world times without number, and will perpetually bring him back until he has severed every link and obtained for himself liberty and emancipation.

It is here that we touch on one of the chief difficulties in understanding the system propounded by Gautama. The doctrine of Metempsychosis, as

[1] Mahâvagga I., 6, 19—22; Mahâ-Parinibbâna-Sutta ii. 2, 3; Dhamma-Kakka-Ppavattana-Sutta, 5—8.

taught by the Brāhmans or by Pythagoras, is perfectly intelligible.   It is a shrewd theory to
account for the inequalities in human life and
destiny.   It fails in this respect, that in order to
satisfy the requirements of the case, the soul that
has transmigrated should be able to recollect
whence it had come, and why its present condition
had been allotted to it.   When Wordsworth
says :—

> " Our birth is but a sleep and a forgetting ;
>   The soul that rises with us, our life's star,
>   Hath had elsewhere its setting
>   And cometh from afar ;
>   Not in entire forgetfulness,
>   And not in utter nakedness,
>   But trailing clouds of glory do we come
>   From God, who is our home," [1]

we cannot but feel that there is more truth in
the "forgetting" than in the absence of the "entire
forgetfulness," and that those seemingly mystic
memories, while capable of another explanation,
are, however they are regarded, wholly inadequate
as a foundation for such a theory.

But the doctrine of transmigration, or rather
of rebirth as taught by Gautama, is weighted
by additional difficulties : for his doctrine was not
Metempscychosis for this reason, that he had no
belief in the existence of a human soul.   Later
Buddhist teachers revert largely to the doctrine of
the Brāhmans on the subject, but the evidence of
the Sacred Books is unmistakable as to the attitude
of Gautama himself.

[1] Ode on Intimations of Immortality.

The nearest approach in his system to what corresponds with the soul is to be found in viññāna or consciousness. But this is one of the five elements of being which are distinctly characterized as changeful and impermanent, and incapable of surviving the shock of death. If, however, the Buddhist creed admits no soul, the question presents itself at once, How is transmigration possible? If every element in human nature be subject to the law of impermanence how can rebirth be effected? What is the constant factor in the successive appearances? I do not think that any conclusion is possible save that in order to be consistent Gautama should have abandoned absolutely the transmigration theory. But this would not only have involved surrendering a conception deeply rooted in the Oriental mind, it would further have deprived the system of a strong motive power to induce men to free themselves from the fetters of sense and sin. There was, however, an alternative which presented itself, namely, to invent some substitute for a soul. Gautama chose this course : in place of a soul he put what is called Karma. The word originally meant " doing " or " action " : and was subsequently used to express " a religious or ecclesiastical act " or " moral merit." In its technical sense it came to signify " a potent cause or energy whereby the multitudinous beings that people the universe are brought into existence." The sum total of the actions of an individual during his lifetime constitute the Karma. When a man dies the elements of his

being perish, but by the force of his Karma a new
set of elements instantly start into existence, and
a new being appears in another world, who, though
possessing a different form and different elements
of being, is in reality identical with the man just
passed away because his Karma is the same.[1] It
is the link that preserves the identity of a being
through all the countless changes which he undergoes.

Strange and well nigh unintelligible as this
theory seems, it is nevertheless possible, I believe,
to get at the real thought that moulded Gautama's
conception. Action of every kind he regarded as
possessing the nature of seed sown: men were found
to some extent to reap the consequences of their
actions during their lifetime: but this takes place
only in a limited and incomplete sense during the
existence to which the actions belong. At the
close of a life many acts remain like seed sown
but not yet grown up. Hence the theory that when
a man dies he leaves the sum total of the acts of
his life as a kind of complex seed, made up of good
and bad elements, which by his death springs up
into a fresh existence, the same, and yet not the
same; in somewhat of the sense in which it might
be said that ordinary seed which springs up is
identical and yet not identical with that which
is sown. Viewed in this light the theory loses its
apparent absurdity. It becomes in fact a mode of
expressing partly what we understand by the Law
of Heredity, which involves a transference of

[1] Childers' *Pali Dictionary*, s. v., Kammam.

character, and a reproduction of the consequences of actions; and partly the Law of Retribution that "Whatsoever a man soweth that shall he also reap." But nevertheless the theory fails in this respect that it is necessary either to interpret the Karma in a grossly materialistic sense, by attributing a real existence to the sum total of the life's actions, and this Gautama would have indignantly repudiated, or else Karma must be regarded as equivalent to the soul or ego, and this also he would have declined to admit. However the Karma theory be regarded, there is no escape from the conclusion that Gautama's system logically necessitated the abandonment of the doctrine of transmigration, and that its retention in the form of rebirth involved difficulties and inconsistencies which resulted in some of his followers gliding back before long into the metempsychosis of the Brāhmans, while others set themselves to elaborate a complicated system of metaphysical speculation, in order thereby to endeavour to evade the force of the objections which their opponents were ready to cast in their teeth.

It is a matter of uncertainty how far back the metaphysical element in Buddhism is to be put; a considerable portion of this division in the Sacred Books is probably of far later date than the time of Gautama. And yet it can hardly have been otherwise than that the germs of this part of the system existed from the first. The speculative bent of the Eastern mind, the prevalent philosophy of the existing Hindu schools of thought, the obvious

surface difficulties belonging to the scheme propounded by Gautama, all make it probable that he
was something more than a teacher of practical
duty. And, whereas there were many abstract
problems that he declined to discuss as being either
unprofitable or insoluble, yet his theory concerning
rebirth of itself made it necessary for him to enter
into the consideration of the elements of human
nature and the laws by which the life of man
is governed and conditioned.[1]

It will be remembered that personal existence
was regarded by the Brāhmans as resulting from
the severance of the Atmān in the individual from
the Atmān of the Universe; and that Ignorance
was an operating agent in occasioning the
severance. There is here a point of contact between
Brāhmanism and Buddhism; for the first link in
Gautama's chain of causation was declared by him
to be Ignorance. But he assigned to the word a
different meaning from that which was given to it
by the Brāhmans. For he held it to signify
ignorance of the four noble truths which he proclaimed. An individual asks, "Why do I now
exist?" Gautama would answer, "You exist

[1] Comp. Burnouf, *Introduction à l'Histoire du Buddhisme
Indien*, p. 405: "En premier lieu, il est utile de savoir si en
effet Çâkya mêlait à ses prédications, dont le charactère le
plus apparent est celui d'une pure morale, l'exposition ou
tout au moins l'indication des principes plus généraux par
lesquels il devait résoudre les grands problèmes de l'existence
de Dieu, de la nature, de l'esprit et de la matière. J'ai, quant
à moi, la conviction qu'il ne sépara jamais la métaphysique
de la morale, et qu'il réunit toujours dans le même enseigne-
ment ces deux parties de la philosophie antique."

now because in your previous state of existence
you were in ignorance of the truths concerning
suffering, its cause, its extinction, and the mode by
which it can be brought to an end." He asks
again, "Why am I what I am?" Gautama
would reply, "You are what you are as the result
of what you were. Your Karma, the sum total
of your actions, has operated under the influence
of Upádána, or cleaving to existence. The latter
force brings you back to life; the former deter-
mines the manner of your life." So it has been, so
it will be times without number; as long as the
Karma and Upádána continue, so long must the
individual be born and reborn. The fetters must be
broken and the chain severed that links the individual to life. Desire must be extinguished in him who
wishes sorrow to end, the recurring series of births
and deaths to cease, and eternal rest to begin.

It may be of interest to know how the
obvious difficulty to which I have referred,
namely, the severance of the links between one
existence and another, was met by the early
Buddhists. In a book which dates from the first
century B.C., and which purports to be a dialogue
between Milinda, King of Ságal, probably an
Asiatic Greek,[1] and Nágasena, a Buddhist sage,
we find the king starting this difficulty. "Then
if the same mind and body is not again produced
or conceived, that being is delivered from the con-

[1] He is identified with Menander, King of Baktria, who
reigned from about B.C. 140 to about B.C. 110. See Introduction to Rhys Davids' translation of *The Questions of King
Milinda* (*S.B.E.*, Vol. XXXV., p. xxiii).

sequences of sinful actions." Nágasena replies, "How so? If there be no future birth there is deliverance; but if there be a future birth deliverance does not necessarily follow. Thus, a man steals a number of mangos, and takes them away; but he is seized by the owner, who brings him before the king and says, 'Sire, this man has stolen my mangos.' But the robber replies, 'I have not stolen his mangos; the mango he set in the ground was one, these mangos are other and different from that. I do not deserve to be punished.' Now, your Majesty, would this plea be valid; would no punishment be deserved?" The king answered, "He would certainly deserve punishment, because, whatever he may say, the mangos he stole were the product of the mango originally set by the man from whom they were stolen, and therefore punishment ought to be inflicted." Thereupon Nágasena said, "In like manner, by means of the Karma produced by this mind and body, another mind and body is caused. There is therefore no deliverance (in this way) from the consequences of sinful actions."[1]

This theory furnished one of the great motive powers by which Buddhist teachers worked. It does not appear that much use was originally made of the threat that an unworthy man would come back to the world under the form of one of the lower animals, but an appeal was made, grounded on the

[1] Spence Hardy, *Manual of Buddhism*, p. 445. The translation by Rhys Davids, which had not been published when the Lectures were written, is more accurate. He substitutes "name and form" for "mind and body."

F

dread of being reborn in one of the innumerable
hells or places of punishment.   I do not think that
it is generally recognised how largely this element
entered into Buddhist teaching.   But even in one
of their ancient Sacred Books we find a detailed description of the torments of sinners. " Our
deeds are not lost," so we read, " they will surely
come (back to you), (their) master will meet them.
The fool who commits sin will feel the pain in himself in the other world.   To the place where one is
struck with iron rods, to the iron stake with sharp
edges he goes ; then there is (for him) food as
appropriate, resembling a hot ball of iron. . . . .
They lie on spread embers ; they enter a blazing
pyre ; covering them with a net they kill them
(there) with iron hammers ; they go to dense darkness, for that is spread out like the body of the
earth.   Then they enter an iron pot ; they enter a
a blazing pyre : for they are boiled in those (iron
pots) for a long time, jumping up and down in the
pyre.   Then he who commits sin is surely boiled
in a mixture of matter and blood, whatever quarter
he inhabits he becomes rotten there from coming in contact (with matter and blood). . . . .
Again, they enter the sharp Asipattavana with
mangled limbs, having seized the tongue with a
hook, the different watchmen (of hell) kill them.
. . . Miserable indeed is the life here (in hell),
which a man sees that commits sin.   Therefore
should a man in this world, for the rest of his life,
be strenuous and not indolent. . . . . As long as
hells are called painful in this world, so long

people will have to live there for a long time. Therefore, amongst those who have pure, amiable, and good qualities one should always guard speech and mind."[1]

It is quite true that these hells are more properly purgatories whither the sinner goes to suffer for his evil deeds:[2] but it must be noted that the duration of existence there was terribly prolonged, and the chance of escape reduced to a minimum, as the following illustration shows, "A man throws a perforated yoke into the sea. The winds blow it in different directions. In the same sea there is a blind tortoise which, after the lapse of a hundred, a thousand, or a hundred thousand years, rises to the surface of the water. Will the time ever come when that tortoise shall so rise up that its neck shall enter the hole of the yoke? It may: but the time that would be required for the happening of this chance cannot be told, and it is equally difficult for the unwise being that has once entered any of the great hells to obtain birth as man."[3]

I may here remark that of such a doctrine as the forgiveness of sins, Buddhism knows absolutely nothing.

The doctrine of a God or Gods by whose providence all things are ordered, Gautama rejected. He substituted Law in their stead: and putting

---

[1] Sutta-Nipâta, 666—678 (*S.B.E.*, Vol. X., p. 123).

[2] Childers lays great stress on this point. *Pali Dictionary*, s. v., Narako.

[3] Quoted by Spence Hardy, *Manual*, p. 459.

the lives and destinies of men under the dominion
of inexorable and inplacable laws the idea of
pardon necessarily vanished. "Be sure your sin
will find you out" is a constant text of Buddhist
discourses.

But side by side with the proclamation of the
certain consequences of wrong-doing, there was
preached the method of deliverance. For whereas
there was (as I have said) no place for forgiveness
in the system, there was a path opened by which
men could be delivered from sorrow and enter into
rest. The great object that had to be effected was
to sever the bonds which united the individual to
existence. According to Gautama there were ten
fetters which had to be broken before this
severance could take place. They are (1) The
delusion of Self (that is of the reality and perma-
nence of the ego); (2) Doubt (specially in regard
to the Buddha and the doctrines which he proclaimed); (3) Reliance on the efficacy of rites and
sacrifices; (4) The bodily lusts and passions;
(5) Hatred and illfeeling; (6) Desire for a future
life in the worlds of form; (7) Desire for a future
life in the formless worlds; (8) Pride; (9) Self-
righteousness; (10) Ignorance.[1] When anyone
has severed the first three fetters, he is regarded as
one who has been, so to speak, converted; he has
accepted the four Noble Truths; he has entered
upon the true path; his ultimate deliverance is
secure; he will be reborn only seven times. The
second stage is marked by a partial rupture of the

[1] *S.B.E.*, Vol. XI., p. 222.

next two fetters—those who get thus far will return once only to the earth and then be reborn once in the heavens. In the third stage those same two fetters are finally sundered, and then there will be but rebirth once in the heavenly worlds. The fourth stage is that of Arahats, or Saints, by them the remaining five fetters are broken.[1] Sorrow, delusion, and evil of every kind are now at an end; the chain has been parted by which they were bound to existence. The Arahat has now but to live out the remainder of his life; and then he will enter that which is for him his perfect consummation and bliss, namely Nirvâna, the final goal.

No language could be found too strong to describe the intense craving after this final rest of the storm-tossed traveller on the sea of life. It was the *summum bonum*, the response to the aspirations of his inmost soul. I quote some of the verses of the Dhammapada in illustration of this, " These wise people, meditative, steady, always possessed of strong powers attain to Nirvâna, the highest happiness."[2] "Some people are born again; evil-doers go to hell; righteous people go to heaven; those who are free from all worldly desires attain Nirvâna."[3] " Health is the greatest of gifts; contentedness, the best riches; trust is the best of relationships; Nirvâna, the highest happiness."[4]

[1] Spence Hardy, *Eastern Monachism*, p. 280; Rhys Davids, *Buddhism*, p. 108.
[2] Dh. 23.   [3] Dh. 126.   [4] Dh. 204.

The question naturally arises—In what did Nirvâna consist?

It was no new word coined by Gautama to be the expression of a dogma peculiar to his system; it was rather one of the many terms which he adopted from pre-existing schools of philosophy. According to the Brâhmans, the individual soul was separated from the World Spirit, and thereby became the victim of sorrow and of change. To overcome this severance was the great aim; reabsorption into the infinite was the final goal; to express this reabsorption they used the word Nirvâna.

Gautama adopted the term which he found ready to his hand, but rejecting the idea of the World Spirit and the whole theory of the Brâhmans touching the soul, it became necessary for him to alter the connotation of the term. The altered signification given to the word has occasioned one of the chief differences of opinion amongst students of Buddhism. Some hold that by Nirvâna, Gautama meant absolute annihilation, the extinction of existence, the final end of life. Others believe that he intended to convey only the obliteration of all evil, all desire, all that goes to make up the sorrow of life; and that Nirvâna is a state of perfect calm and peace, where the changes and chances of this mortal life can never enter, where the weary have eternal and unbroken rest. The difficulty of deciding between the two views may be seen by tracing the mental changes through which such a thinker as Max Müller has passed in reference to this subject. In 1857 he published a pamphlet. entitled, "Buddhism and Buddhist Pilgrims," in which he thus explains the final goal of Buddhism. "There is no deliverance from evil except by breaking through the prison walls not only of life but of existence, and by extirpating the cause of existence," and he further quotes the following passage from the dialogue between Milinda and Nágasena. *Mil.*—"Then can you point out to me the place in which he is?" *Nág.*—"Our Bhagavat has attained Nirvâna, where there is no repetition of birth. We cannot say that he is here, or that he is there. When a fire is extinguished can it be said that it is here or that it is there? Even so our Buddha has attained extinction. He is like the sun that has set behind the Astigiri mountain. It cannot be said that he is here or that he is there, but we can point him out by the discourses he delivered; in them he lives."[1]

But some years later, in a preface to a translation of the Dhammapada, Max Müller takes a different view. "Nirvâna," he writes, "may mean the extinction of many things—of selfishness, desire and sin, without going so far as the extinction of personal consciousness. Further, if we consider that Buddha himself, after he had already seen Nirvâna, still remains on earth until his body falls a prey to death. That in the legends Buddha appears to his disciples even after his death, it seems to me that all these circumstances are hardly reconcilable with the orthodox meta-

[1] *Buddhism and Buddhist Pilgrims*, p. 53.

physical doctrine of Nirvâna."[1]   His view, therefore, at that time, was that, according to the
original teaching of Gautama, Nirvâna meant
"the entering of the soul into rest," and that the
doctrine of annihilation was a perversion of later
times.

I am not aware that Max Müller has formally
abandoned this view ; but I gather from the notes
to his more recent translation of the Dhammapada
in the "Sacred Books of the East," that he has
found that it cannot be maintained, and that,
though evidently most reluctantly, he has been
obliged to revert to the original idea of annihilation.[2]

A great deal of the difficulty connected with this
subject arises from the fact that there are two
apparently opposite sets of expression used in the
Buddhist books about Nirvâna.   In some places
it is described as a condition of happiness, of joy
and peace ; in others it is spoken of as extinction.
The explanation of this consists in what is often
lost sight of, namely, that, according to Buddhist
teaching, the state of Nirvâna is reached prior to
death.   Thus, in the case of Gautama himself, he
attained Nirvâna under the Bo-tree at the conclusion of his spiritual struggle ; but he remained
on earth for forty-five years after, until his existence
came to an end.   And this is his teaching with
regard to his followers also.   Those who have

[1] *Buddhagosha's Parables*, by Capt. T. Rogers and Prof.
Max Müller, Preface, p. xli.

[2] Dhammapada 23 (*S.B.E.*, Vol. X., p. 9).

attained the fourth stage of the path, who have broken the ten fetters and become Arahats, or Saints, they have attained Nirvâna.

In fact, notwithstanding the marvellous contrast, there is a certain parallelism between our conception of Eternal Life and the Buddhist teaching as to Nirvâna. We believe Eternal Life to consist in spiritual union between Christ and the human soul ; he in whom this union exists " hath eternal life," a life over which death has no power.[1] This Life that endures for ever is received during this state of existence, and when this state of existence closes then comes the consummation and full realisation of the Life ; what St. Paul calls the tent dwelling is cast off—the soul enters its eternal abode.[2]

So Gautama taught ; the chains that fetter the individual and bring him back times without number to existence must be severed here ; when they are severed the final deliverance and emancipation of the individual are secure ; he lives out his life as a liberated being and then his consummation is received, namely, absolute and everlasting nothingness. Those expressions, therefore, that describe Nirvâna as a condition of happiness and peace, refer to the life of the saint who has attained the exalted condition of freedom from all the fetters. The expressions on the other hand that speak of Nirvâna as extinction, refer to the climax when existence itself is at an end.

For that absolute annihilation was the original

[1] St. John vi. 47, viii. 51, xi. 25, 26.　　[2] 2 Cor. v. 1.

Buddhist idea attached to the word Nirvâna seems
to me the only conclusion that can be drawn from
the language of the Sacred Books.   The following
quotations, in illustration of this, are taken from
the Discourses—" The old is destroyed, the new
has not arisen ; those whose minds are disgusted
with a future existence, the wise who have
destroyed their seeds (of existence and) whose
desires do not increase, go out like this lamp."[1]
" Who, except the noble, deserve the well-under-
stood state of Nirvâna ?   Having perfectly conceived this state, those free from passion are
completely extinguished."[2]   " For those who stand
in the middle of the water, so said the venerable
Kappa, in the formidable stream that has set in,
for those who are overcome by decay and death,
tell me of an island that this pain may not again
come on."   " This matchless island," Buddha
replied, " possessing nothing and grasping at
nothing, I call Nirvâna, the destruction of decay
and death."[3]

What is thus clearly expressed in the Buddhist
Books is moreover a necessary part of the system
itself.   It is important to emphasize this fact, as
on the testimony of the Books alone it would
not be possible to refute Max Müller's idea that
annihilation, as an interpretation of Nirvâna, was
an invention of Gautama's disciples and not the
doctrine of the great Teacher himself.   If, how-

[1] Kúlavagga 234 (S.B.E., Vol. X., p. 39).
[2] Mahâvagga 765 (S.B.E., Vol. X., p. 145).
[3] Pârâyanavagga 1091, 1092 (S.B.E., Vol. X., 203).

ever, it is an essential part of the system, that line of argument falls to the ground. And Gautama taught that existence was an evil: this is expressed as an unqualified assertion: neither on earth nor in the heavenly worlds—neither men nor Devas have an untroubled life: hence in the extinction of existence alone can rest be found. Thus we can understand how he teaches that the Gods or Devas themselves envy the man who has attained the blissful state of Nirvâna.

Nor would it be easy—on the theory that Nirvâna meant anything but annihilation—to define what in the nature of man could exist in that state. The elements of existence are broken up—consciousness comes to an end—there is no soul or supersensuous element admitted in the system — the Karma which forms the connecting link between different existences is destroyed—what then can Nirvâna mean but absolute extinction?[1]

It is the horror of the idea that has made so many look out for any other possible interpretation of the word. In fact Max Müller plainly states that it is his repugnance to such a goal as the *summum bonum* that made him reluctant to ascribe such a dogma to Gautama, and rather to view it as an invention of his followers. But it was in reality the reverse process that took place: for the Northern Buddhists broke away from the original teaching of the founder of the system and glided into a belief in immortality and in a

[1] See Appendix III.

heaven so sensuous that it is hard to understand how they can consistently call themselves
Buddhists.

It is a fact we should not have anticipated in the
religious history of the world that a leader of men
such as Gautama could have set before his followers
as their aim, so to live that they might inherit everlasting nothingness.

In this connection I cannot forbear from calling
attention to one of the strangest comments I have
met in the study of Buddhism. In the article on
Nirvâna in his Pali Dictionary Childers discusses
the subject most clearly and powerfully. There is
no source I am acquainted with where it is possible
to learn more of the facts bearing upon the
different views that have been held. And yet
towards the close of the article he writes, "It is
not my intention here to discuss the ethical aspect
of the question of Nirvâna, and I shall content
myself with observing that Christianity with its
doctrine of everlasting punishment can ill afford to
reproach Buddhism with a doctrine of annihilation."
That is, in other words, because we believe in what
is intended to act as a terrible warning, we can
say nothing about what Buddhism teaches as a
thing most to be desired. What Christianity
entreats men to keep from, is set as parallel to what
Buddhism bids them strive after.

It is not a question of reproach ; but if the two
systems are weighed against each other, we cannot
but feel that there is something unspeakably
dreary—something that conflicts with the deepest

and highest aspirations of our nature—in setting before men as the ideal of human life, so to live that they may attain the reward of annihilation. And in contrast there is what is both most cheering and ennobling in the hope set before us by Him whom we follow and adore; the hope that assures us that if this world has its shadows and its sorrows there is a nobler and a higher life where every part of our nature shall be completely developed, and every aspiration of our heart fully realized—a life where there shall be work without weariness and service free from distraction—where clouds and darkness shall have vanished and everlasting light shall shine—where peace and rest and joy and love shall abide for evermore, and God shall be all in all.

LECTURE V.

MICAH vi. 8.—" He hath showed thee, O man, what is good ;
and what doth the Lord require of thee, but to do justly, and
to love mercy, and to walk humbly with thy God."

BUDDHISM may be fitly termed a system, or even a
creed : but unless the word is used in a very ex-
tended sense, it is impossible to call it a religion.
With us, religion is so inseparably connected with
our duty towards God, that the one thought
immediately suggests the other. Even Schleier-
macher's vague definition of religion, that it consists in a feeling of dependence, excludes such a
system as Buddhism ; for one of its keynotes is
self-dependence, " Rouse thyself by thyself,
examine thyself by thyself, thus, self-protected and
attentive, wilt thou live happily, O Bhikshu ;
for self is the lord of self, self is the refuge of self :
therefore curb thyself as a merchant curbs a good
horse."[1] " Be ye lamps unto yourselves. Betake
yourselves to no external refuge. Look not for
refuge to any one but yourselves."[2] A system,
moreover, which regards belief in a Personal God
as " only a gigantic shadow thrown upon the void
of space by the imagination of ignorant men,"[3]

Dhammapada 379, 380.   [2] Mahâ-Parinibbâna-Sutta ii. 33.
[3] Olcott's *Buddhist Catechism*, p. 29.

which admits no higher Powers (for the Devas of Buddhism are inferior to the Saints, and come to learn from them), which as a necessary consequence refuses to recognise any efficacy in religious rites and ceremonies, in sacrifices or in prayers—such a system excludes so much that we connect with the term religion, that we feel far more like dealing with a philosophy than with a creed.

It is hard to realize how teaching which thus admitted no God, no prayer, no sacrifices, no ceremonial, and whose goal was annihilation, could gain or retain any hold over the minds of men.

The key to the difficulty lies in the Order which Gautama founded. What his system lacked in dogma, he endeavoured to supply by means of discipline.[1]

It is a singular coincidence that Buddhism has its ten commandments — some of them identical with those which we hold to bind ourselves.

They may be expressed briefly as follows:

[1] Comp. Burnouf, *Introduction à l'Histoire du Buddhisme Indien*, p. 300 : " Qu'est-ce en effet que la Discipline pour un corps de Religieux, si ce n'est l'ensemble des prescriptions qui assurent et régularisent la pratique des devoirs? Et si ces devoirs sont en grande partie de ceux que la morale impose, c'est-à-dire de ceux auquels la conscience humaine reconnaît un charactère obligatoire, la Discipline ne devient-elle pas en quelque sorte la forme de la morale dont elle exprime les arrêts ? Cela est d'antant plus vrai, que les systèmes religieux accordent une part plus considérable à la morale, et une moindre au dogme. Dans de tels systèmes, la Discipline grandit avec la théorie des devoirs dont elle est la sauvegarde, en même temps que le culte décroît avec le dogme dont il exprime les conceptions sous une forme extérieure."

1. Thou shalt not kill. 2. Thou shalt not steal.
3. Thou shalt not tell lies. 4. Thou shalt not
drink intoxicating liquors. 5. Thou shalt not be
guilty of impurity. 6. Thou shalt not eat unseasonable food at nights. 7. Thou shalt not
wear garlands nor use perfumes. 8. Thou shalt
not use a high or a broad bed. 9. Thou shalt abstain
from dancing, singing, music, and stage plays.
10. Thou shalt not receive gold nor silver. Whereas,
however, the Ten Commandments originally delivered to the Israelites were made universally
obligatory, Gautama drew a distinction as to
the binding force of his precepts.

At the root of the Buddhist conception of the
higher life lay the thought of the necessity of
separation from the world. As Gautama himself
had forsaken his palace and his father's home,
so he taught that those who desired emancipation from the sorrows of existence must
renounce all that they had. But he had too keen
an insight into human nature to confine his system
to such only as were willing thus absolutely to
surrender themselves. And as celibacy was an
essential condition of admission to the Order, its
duration would have been imperilled had no place
been found for persons who were unwilling to under-
take all the obligations laid upon those who were
admitted within its fellowship. Hence there
was founded an order of lay disciples—house-
holders who retained their original mode of
life and yet undertook the fulfilment of certain
precepts imposed on them by the Teacher. They

were bound by the first five commandments—
that is, to abstain from murder, theft, falsehood, impurity, and the use of intoxicating
drinks. They were recommended to observe,
specially on assembly days and during sacred
seasons, the next three precepts, that is, not
to eat at night unseasonable food, not to wear
wreaths or use perfumes, and to sleep on a mat
spread on the ground. But for them these
precepts were of the nature of " counsels of perfection."

To the lay order male and female members were
admitted alike. Great merit was attached to the
fulfilment of the commands: rebirth in a more
exalted position was secured to those who obeyed
them. Their standing and privileges, however,
were immeasurably inferior to those of the regular
members of the Order of which the Buddhist
Church or Assembly, properly speaking, consisted.
The Assembly was divided into two classes—
novices and fully enrolled members : the ceremony
of initiation is called by many writers " Ordina-
tion," and Childers compares the two classes to
Deacons and Priests.[1] But this suggests a wrong
train of ideas. The parallel to the Buddhist
Assembly is to be found, not in the Christian
Ministry, but rather in the Monastic Orders.
And even here the parallelism is only partial.
Members of the Buddhist Sangha were as free
to leave the community as to join it : there
was no vow of obedience. The novice

[1] Pali Dictionary, s.v. Pabbajjá and Upasampadá.

had a protector or superior, but when the noviciate was ended, he was subordinate to no one.

The term of the noviciate was, as a rule, four months, but it might be longer if the postulant was young. For whereas a novice might be admitted from eight years old and upwards, full membership was limited to those who were at least twenty years of age. The form of admission to the noviciate was very simple ; the presence of a fully enrolled member was alone necessary. The postulant assumed the robes of a dull orange colour, which were the outward and visible sign of membership in the community; his head and beard were shaved, and he thrice reverently repeated the sacred formula, "I take my refuge in the Buddha; I take my refuge in the Law; I take my refuge in the Assembly."[1]

The ceremony of full initiation was more elaborate. It necessitated a chapter meeting or assembly of the mendicants.[2] A series of questions was put, demanding whether the applicant for admission was a human being (not a demon in human shape) ; a male ; twenty years of age ; whether he was a freeman ; without debts ; not afflicted with incurable diseases ; not in the royal service ; and whether his father and mother had given their consent.[3] If the questions were satisfactorily answered, the Assembly formally admitted

[1] Mahâvagga I., 54, 3.
[2] Ten at least being present. Mahâvagga I., 31, 2.
[3] Mahâvagga I., 39—49, 76.

the candidate, and, in doing so, informed him of the rules as to food, residence, dress and medicine, and warned him of the four offences that would result in irrevocable exclusion from the Order, namely, unchastity, theft, murder, and the claiming to himself of any merit or supernatural power.[1] There was a fortnightly meeting of the members of the Order, held on the days of the new moon and full moon.[2] These were days for special observance of the precepts and also of the ceremony of confession, which entered largely into the Buddhist code, as a chief aid for the maintenance of the prescribed discipline. An elaborate list of rules was drawn up, containing a specification of different kinds of offences, and of the penalties or penances which were to follow.[3] At every meeting these rules were recited ; any member who had transgressed was bound to declare his fault. Silence signified innocence. But to remain silent when guilty was regarded as a heinous offence. For certain grave faults the penalty was exclusion from the Order ; but for the majority of transgressions there was imposed a period of probation, which practically meant degradation, varying in length according to the gravity of the offence.

In addition to the fortnightly meeting, the three rainy months, and the month immediately following, were observed as a season of retirement, during which the mendicants intermitted their itinerant

---

[1] *Ibid.*, I., 78.   [2] *Ibid.*, II., 4, 2.
[3] Contained in the Pâtimokkha (*i.e.*, Disburdenment), *S. B. E.*, Vol. XIII.

life and gave themselves up to meditation and a
certain degree of study.   During the rest of the
year they had no fixed abode.   They were taught
to rise early and to live generally a quiet, simple
life. They carried their almsbowl from door to door,
never refusing what was offered to them.   But the
vow of poverty, which they were obliged to take,
was evaded in this way : that whereas no mendicant could accept any gift as a personal offering,
he was permitted to take it as the property of the
Order, and thus, in course of time, great wealth was
accumulated, not to the advantage of the community.

It is scarcely possible for us to conceive such a
life as that of these mendicants, severed from
prayer and devotion, which entered so largely into
the rules of the Monastic Orders.   But prayer was
utterly excluded by the very terms of Gautama's
system.   There was, however, a kind of substitute
for it, namely, certain acts of meditation, which
were prescribed for use at the close of the day and at
dawn.   There was first the meditation of kindness ;
the mendicant was to exercise this wish, " May all
the superior orders of beings be happy ; may they
all be free from sorrow, disease, and evil desire ;
may all men, whether they be mendicants or not,
all the Devas, all who are suffering the pains of
hell, be happy."   One of the chief points insisted
on in this meditation is that all enmity must be
laid aside ; the mendicant is to think of the good
there is in his enemy, that in some   previous

existence his enemy may have toiled for his benefit, or he is to think "What am I at enmity with? is it with the hair or with the bones, or with what?" so that it may have nothing to fasten on. If no other plan prevails he is to make a present to his enemy. In reference to this, it is said "The giving of alms is a blessing to him who receives as well as to him who gives; but the receiver is inferior to the giver." We cannot but recall the words "It is more blessed to give than to receive."[1] The second meditation is compassion—"May the poor be relieved from their indigence and be abundantly supplied." The third is joy—"May the good fortune of the prosperous never pass away; may each one receive his own appointed reward." The fourth meditation is upon the impermanency, the impurity, and unreality of the body. And the last, which is superior to all the others, and practised by the Arahats or Saints, is that of equanimity. In it "all sentient beings are regarded alike, one is not loved more than another, nor hated more than another; towards all there is indifference."[2]

The keynote of Buddhism is struck here: beyond and above every virtue there is set the emotionless frame of mind which neither sorrows nor rejoices, which feels neither hate nor love. It is thus that we are enabled to explain what would otherwise seem an anomaly in Gautama's teaching. If existence be an evil, we might have expected that

[1] Acts xx. 35.
[2] Spence Hardy, *Eastern Monachism*, pp. 243—249

he would have anticipated the recommendation of
some of Schopenhauer's disciples and counselled
suicide as a speedy mode of deliverance.

Suicide was, however, strongly discouraged,
partly on the ground that it would be a loss to the
world if those who were best able to instruct men
were to vanish from the earth; but still more
because suicide implies a desire to die, and the
true Buddhist Saint has no desires. Hence one
of Gautama's principal disciples is reported to
have said, " I am like a servant awaiting the command of his master, ready to obey it, whatever it
may be; I await the appointed time for the cessation of existence; I have no wish to live; I have
no wish to die : desire is extinct."[1]

From such a creed it necessarily followed that no
place could be found for affection or love.   There
are some expressions in the Sacred Books that
seem to point in an opposite direction.   It is said,
for example, "As a mother at the risk of her life
watches over her own child, so also let every one
cultivate a boundless (friendly) mind towards all
beings. And let him cultivate goodwill towards all
the world, a boundless friendly mind above and
below and across, unobstructed, without hatred,
without enmity.   Standing, walking, or sitting or
lying, as long as he is awake, let him devote himself
to this mind : this (way of) living, they say, is the
best in the world."[2] It has been asserted that thus

[1] Spence Hardy, *Eastern Monachism,* p. 287.   The
Questions of King Milinda ii. 2, 4 (*S. B. E.,* Vol. XXXV., p.
70).   See Appendix V.

[2] Sutta-Nipâta, 148—150.

the keynote of Buddhism is identical with that of Christianity. But although the Agapè of the New Testament is moral more than emotional, nevertheless Christian Love as taught by our Lord—as haloed by His example—as eulogised by St. Paul, is essentially opposed to the cold, negative spirit of indifference—the Stoic apatheia—the reflective consequence-calculating principle enjoined in Buddhism. The most sacred bonds that unite man to man—the ties of home life and of affectionate friendship were absolutely condemned as hindrances to spiritual progress ; and no place was found for a Being who might alike be adored and loved with all the heart and all the strength and all the mind.

Closely allied with this subject there may be mentioned another guiding principle of Buddhism, namely its spirit of toleration towards those who adopted a different creed.

In one of the pillar edicts of King Asoka we find the following prayer, " I pray with every variety of prayer for those who differ from me in creed that they, following after my proper example, may with me attain unto eternal salvation." Another edict gives this as a description of true religion, " This is the true religious devotion, this the sum of religious instruction, that it should increase the mercy and charity, the truth and purity, the kindness and honesty of the world."[1] There are, however, various motives that lead to tolera-

[1] Cunningham, *Corpus Inscriptionum Indicarum*, Vol. I. Edicts vi. and viii.

tion.[1] And in the case of Buddhism, I do not think
that there is any lack of charity in ascribing its
toleration partly to the predominant spirit of
indifference, and still more to a kind of conscious
superiority : if other men were not as they were,
it was their own loss: they merited not persecution,
but pity.

It might seem that in such a system no place could
be found for any conception of sin : nor is there
if we use the word in the sense of a transgression of
a Divine law. Interpreted, however, as signifying
evil seed or evil tendencies, sin holds a prominent
position. Buddhism recognises ten sins, namely,
murder, theft, adultery (sins of act), lying, slander,
abuse, unprofitable conversation (sins of word),
covetousness, malice, scepticism (sins of thought).[2]
The root conception attached to the thought of sin
is, as we might suppose, that sooner or later it is
certain to do the sinner harm, " If a man commits
a sin, let him not do it again ; let him not delight
in sin: pain is the outcome of evil. Even an evildoer sees happiness as long as his deed has not
ripened ; but when his evil deed has ripened, then
does the evildoer see evil. Let no man think
lightly of evil, saying in his heart, it will not come
nigh unto me. Even by the falling of water
drops a waterpot is filled ; the fool becomes full of

[1] Comp. Kuenen, Hibbert Lectures, *National and Universal
Religions*, p. 290: " Let us reflect that Buddhism would never
have been, as it was, toleration itself, had it been any less
sceptical and quietistic."

[2] Spence Hardy, *Manual of Buddhism*, p. 477.

evil, even if he gather it little by little.   Let a man avoid evil deeds, as a merchant, if he has few companions and carries much wealth, avoids a dangerous road ; as a man who loves life avoids poison.   Not in the sky, not in the midst of the sea, not if we enter into the clefts of the mountains, is there known a spot in the whole world where a man might be freed from an evil deed."[1]

In contrast with what men were thus warned to avoid, we may set what they were bidden to strive after.   They were taught that the four greatest virtues were truth, self-restraint, liberality, and forbearance.   Hypocrisy in every form was severely condemned : in language that closely resembles our Lord's description of the Pharisees of His day, we find the warning given, "He who wishes to put on the yellow dress without having cleansed himself from sin, who disregards also temperance and truth, is unworthy of the yellow dress.   What is the use of platted hair, O fool ; what of the raiment of goatskins ?   Within thee there is ravening, but the outside thou makest clean."[2]   Before any good could be done to others they were taught they must conquer self, "Let each man direct himself first to what is proper, then let him teach others ; thus a wise man will not suffer.   If a man make himself as he teaches others to be, then being himself well subdued, he may subdue others ; one's own self is indeed

[1] Dhammapada, 117, 119, 121, 123, 127.
[2] *Ibid.*, 9, 394.

difficult to subdue."[1] There is one verse contained
in the Dhammapada which is regarded by the
Buddhists themselves as a brief but solemn summary of their Master's teaching, " Not to commit
any sin; to do good, and to purify one's mind,
this is the teaching of (all) the Awakened."[2]

It is impossible to study the moral precepts of
Buddhism without being struck both by their
beauty and by the knowledge they manifest of the
human heart.   Much of what is most wonderful in
them must be attributed to Gautama himself. And
when we recall alike the age in which he lived, and
the surroundings amidst which he grew up, it is all
the more remarkable that he should have soared to
such a height. He has been compared to Socrates ;
and the parallel partly holds. But Socrates did
not leave his impress upon Greece, not to say
Europe, to anything like the extent to which
Gautama influenced Asia.   We may freely confess
that from his teaching there is much that Christians of the nineteenth century may profitably learn.
I lay stress on this because of the defects in Buddhism, as a system of ethics that I have now to
notice. These criticisms are not the outcome of
inability to appreciate what is true and beautiful
in that creed ; nor of the narrow-mindedness that
would refuse to recognise that light and truth are
to be found elsewhere, as well as with ourselves.
But when it is asserted that Buddhism may be set
side by side with Christianity, as equally true in

[1] *Ibid.*, 158, 159.   [2] *Ibid.*, 183.

its standards of duty and its precepts of life—nay, more, when some claim for it a superiority to our own belief, then there is thrown down a challenge which it is impossible not to accept. Christianity need not fear the comparison : for when we contrast the two systems there appear in Buddhism defects and omissions that not only deprive it of the position of a religion, which in reality it does not profess to be, but also of the claim to supply a true basis for the government of human life and conduct.

Now, the starting-point of Buddhism is sorrow —the necessary and inseparable connection between sorrow and existence. A man's moral nature must be in an unhealthy condition that cannot recognize that if human life has its dark side, it has also its joy and brightness ; and that there are few, if any, human beings in whose existence light does not predominate over darkness. But Buddhism refuses any brightness to life. It says to those who are prosperous and contented, " You think yourself happy, but the thought is in itself a proof that you are really unhappy, for you are the victim of delusion, in that you have not recognised the sacred truth concerning sorrow." And even on this basis note how it acts. If there were any persons to whom the message of Buddhism ought to have been sent, it was to those who were afflicted with incurable diseases. To them, it might have been expected that the door of hope would have been opened, and the prospect of deliverance held out as a solace to their woes. Instead of this they found themselves ruthlessly thrust away : they were refused admission to the Order : they were told that they were suffering the consequences of their misdeeds, and that until they returned to the world in an existence in which their disease would have passed away, no hope could be held out before them.[1] Christianity does not base itself upon the sorrow, but upon the sin of the world : behind the external disorder it teaches that there is a disturbing cause in human nature, but nevertheless it has its message for sufferers of every kind, " Come unto Me all ye that labour and are heavy laden, and I will give you rest."[2]

If a leper came to Gautama, he must needs send him away as unworthy of admission to his community. When lepers came to Christ, they found their request for healing met with the ready response, " I will, be thou clean."

But, further, Buddhism apparently teaches self-sacrifice, and yet, in reality, the whole system is based upon selfish considerations. You are forbidden to do wrong, but the motive power is that wrong-doing will, sooner or later, be productive to you of pain. You are commanded to do right, but it is in order that you may thereby accomplish your own deliverance. You are told to be liberal, but it is because liberality will certainly meet with its reward. You are directed not to indulge in enmity towards your neighbour, but the reason is that were you to do so you would be doing an injury to

[1] Mahâvagga I., 39.   [2] St. Matthew xi. 28.

yourself. In fact the whole system is a calculation founded upon the dictates of policy—the supreme question in every case is—Will this be to my advantage ?

This criticism may, however, be met with the retort that Christianity does precisely the same, and that the reward of heaven and fear of hell occupy in our religion the same place that the striving after Nirvàna has for the Buddhist. I do not think the retort is justifiable, mainly for this reason : that neither heaven nor hell are *motives* with us, they are rather *results*. The difference is essential. A man who would set going to heaven before him as his aim, would be absolutely certain to fail, because, if the motive be the consideration of happiness, the immediate and tangible would certainly prevail over the distant and spiritual, and the pleasures of sin would therefore triumph over the aspirations for heaven. We teach that heaven is a reward and an encouragement, but that the motive for right doing should be higher and stronger than that of going to heaven, namely, the desire to do the will of the Eternal Father from whom alone all good things do come, and the constraining power of the love of Christ, who died for us that we should no longer live unto ourselves, but unto Him who loved us and gave Himself for us.

I have said that Buddhism seems to be exclusively founded on considerations of policy— closely connected with this is the fact that it supplies no true conception of duty, nor, indeed, any

real notion of right and wrong.   The noble scorn
of consequences which animates the man whose
mind is imbued with the eternal and unchangeable
laws of right and duty—the spirit which led the
youths at Babylon to cry " Our God, whom we
serve, is able to deliver us, and He will deliver us
out of thy hand, O King.   But if not, be it known
unto thee, that we will not serve thy gods, nor
worship the graven image which thou hast set up," [1]
—this spirit has no place in the Buddhist system.
For scorn of consequences it inculcated calculation
of consequences, for disinterested devotion to duty
it substituted prudent regard to personal emancipation.   Even the corporate life of the Buddhist
Brotherhood did not free the system from the
narrowing tendency of individual interest.   Each
member of the Order lived to himself; there was
little, if any, opportunity given for mutual
encouragement and help, in fact such an idea was
opposed to the self-dependence which Gautama
so strongly urged.   We read of acts of self-sacrifice
for the good of the world—but the stories in which
these acts are detailed are either imaginary incidents in non-actual existences, or else they are
rounded with the record of the fruit they bore to
the individual who performed them, so as to prove
that the virtue had its own reward.   So far as I
know we look in vain in the records of Buddhism
for any trace of the true spirit of self-sacrifice that
finds expression in the prayer of Moses, " Now, if
Thou wilt forgive their sin—and if not, blot me, I

[1] Daniel iii. 17, 18.

pray Thee, out of Thy book,"[1]—and in the words of St. Paul, " I could wish that myself were anathema from Christ for my kinsmen, my brethren according to the flesh."[2] I do no more than mention that greatest act of Divine self-sacrifice, absolutely unexampled and unparalleled, on the part of Him, who came not to be ministered unto but to minister, and to give His life a ransom for many.[3]

If it be asked whether does Buddhism or Christianity set forth the truer conception of human nature, and the nobler ideal of human life ? it is hard to see how any but the one answer can be given to the question.

We believe that our nature has come to us from God, and that body, soul, and spirit, all our powers and energies, can be sanctified by His Spirit and consecrated to His service.

Buddhism teaches that men have neither soul nor spirit, that the body is a mass of pollution and corruption, that the affections and emotions are but delusive ties and sorrow-causing fetters, that from first to last the supreme effort of the intelligent should be to crush and repress their nature until they have purified themselves from all taint of desire and made themselves the cold, passionless, emotionless beings, in which its ideal is realized and due preparation made for the consummation of extinction.

We hold that whereas there is a germ of truth in this conception, for that there are some tendencies and passions that must be con-

[1] Exod. xxxii. 32.   [2] Romans ix. 3.   [3] St. Matt. xx. 28.

quered if our nature is to attain its destiny and realize the ideal that is set before us, nevertheless our body is something more and better than a mass of corruption, for that it is "the Temple of the Holy Ghost, which is in us, which we have from God," and that therefore we can "glorify God in our body."[1]   We believe that our affections and emotions are to be consecrated rather than repressed : for to us the first of all truths is contained in the declaration that "God is Love,"[2] and the first of all commandments is summed up in the utterance, "Thou shalt love the Lord thy God."[3]   We believe that the soul or mind is the gift of God, and that it is His desire that we should develop and cultivate the mental powers with which He has endowed us, so that we may understand both what is around us and within.   And we find in the will which governs our actions—in the reason which guides our judgments—in the conscience which administers the law of right and wrong, the infallible proof that we have been made in the image of God, and after His likeness: that we are something better therefore than flakes of foam carried round and round in the whirlpool of existence—that we have some nobler aim set before us than merely so to curb our nature that we shall know neither joy nor sorrow, neither hope nor fear—that we have some brighter prospect awaiting us than to fade like the streaks of morning cloud into the infinite

---

[1] 1 Corinthians vi. 19, 20.   [2] 1 St. John iv. 16.
[3] St. Matt. xxii. 37, 38.

azure of everlasting nothingness—that we are the children of God, called to glorify Him on earth by lives of lowly service and of willing obedience and destined hereafter to see Him as He is, and to be made like unto Him in His eternal and everlasting Glory.

LECTURE VI.

St. John viii. 12.—"Then spake Jesus, saying, I am the Light of the World, he that followeth Me shall not walk in darkness, but shall have the Light of Life."

I HAVE had occasion in previous Lectures to refer to some of the parallels between the Sacred Books of the Buddhists and our own Scriptures, and also to points of contact between their teaching and what we acknowledge ourselves. The existence of these parallelisms is by no means a modern discovery. One of the most popular books of the Middle Ages was "The history of Barlaam and Joasaph," ascribed on very creditable authority to St. John of Damascus. This Christian Saint held the office of vizir to the Caliph of Damascus. But in his later years he retired to the monastery of St. Sabas, near Jerusalem, where he died about A.D. 760. At some time during his life he must have come in contact with Buddhists : he read or heard them repeat some of their Sacred Books : he seems to have entered into controversy with them, and in "The History of Barlaam and Joasaph" he gives a summary of the arguments which he employed. We can readily understand with what force the similarities between the Buddhist Order and the Monastic system would at that time strike a thoughtful mind. Earnest Christians then felt keenly the wickedness of the world : it seemed to them that men were bartering eternity for time, and fixing their affections upon what was transitory and vain. To escape surrounding pollution and to attain holiness they believed it necessary to withdraw from the world, to live an ascetic life, to curb their bodily passions, and by self-discipline and self-mortification to attain purity of heart and mind : they practised poverty, celibacy, and contemplation, and living in communities they submitted to the rules and penances imposed on them.

Is it not very natural that a Christian monk of the eighth century, hearing for the first time the tenets of Buddhism, should be struck by the similarities between his own manner of life and that of the mendicants of the East ? So I believe it was in the case of St. John of Damascus. His intention in writing the story was doubtless in part that it might act as an Eirenicon, to show Buddhists how like Christianity was in some respects to what they believed themselves, and partly as a persuasive argument to prove to them that whereas Christianity started from somewhat similar premisses, it led to an infinitely better conclusion. In fact, we may go a step further, and conjecture that the narrative is constructed so as to show how the author believed Gautama himself would have been affected had he been brought into contact with the religion of Christ. For the whole story of Joasaph, the hero of the romance, is an adaptation of the legendary life of the Buddha. Buddhist and Christian phraseology are interwoven most ingeniously throughout the narrative, and many Eastern parables and fables are introduced, but in some cases very inaptly: it is manifest that they are used in a different connection from that which they originally served. One of the strangest circumstances in regard to this romance is that in course of time it came to be looked upon as a record of actual occurrences, and some Pope, it is impossible to say which, inserted the names of Barlaam and Joasaph into the Canon of the Church. The result being that under the name of St. Joasaph the founder of Buddhism is commemorated on November 27th of every year as a Christian Saint by the Roman Catholic Church; and the name of the holy St. Joasaph has also found its way into the Menology of the Greeks.[1]

There are some who maintain that the parallelisms between Christianity and Buddhism are something more than accidental; that previous to the Christian era Palestine was affected with Buddhist ideas—that the sect of the Essenes amongst the Jews adopted many Buddhist tenets and that thus it has had, from the first, a direct influence upon Christianity. It seems to me a question of interest to determine whether this theory can be maintained; it would be both unwise and uncritical to

[1] See Appendix I.

dismiss it without a hearing. I could conceive it as quite in harmony with what we know of our Blessed Lord, that He should have pointed out that there was truth intermingled with Buddhist errors, if He had found the system known and followed by the Jews of His day, and St. Paul was sufficiently broad-minded to appropriate and utilise truth from whencesoever it was derived.

But the first question that presents itself is whether the similarities are sufficient to warrant any theory of intercommunication between the two systems? I do not think they are. An examination of parallelisms between the Buddhist Books and our Scriptures leads me to the conclusion, that on this line of proof, it is quite as possible to argue that the Buddhists borrowed from the Old Testament, as that the early Christians were influenced by Buddhist conceptions. If we were to argue that Gautama derived some of his thoughts from the Book of Proverbs, we know what reception the theory would receive. But Professor Seydel argues in favour of a far more unlikely supposition. He conjectures that one of the "*many*" to whom St. Luke refers as having taken in hand to record the life of Our Lord, wrote a history in which acts and words were attributed to Him that, in reality, belonged to Gautama's legendary story, and that this document influenced not only our Canonical Gospels, but also the fundamental conceptions of the early Christians. We naturally ask " What are the parallelisms upon which such an hypothesis rests ? " One which Professor Seydel describes as

"most noteworthy" is the following.[1] Before his
renunciation of home, Gautama was driving
through the city in a splendid chariot, a maiden
who saw him burst forth into this song of joy
"Blessed indeed is that mother; blessed indeed
is that father; blessed indeed is that wife, who
owns this Lord so glorious." Hearing the song he
thought to himself, "On catching sight of such a
one the heart of his mother, of his father, of his
wife, is made happy! This is all she says. But
by what can every heart attain to lasting happiness
and peace? When the fire of lust, of hatred and
delusion are gone out, when the troubles of mind
arising from pride, credulity, and all other sins have
ceased, then peace is gained. This very day I
will break away from household cares! I will
renounce the world! I will follow only after the
Nirvâna itself." Then loosing from his neck a
string of pearls worth a hundred thousand, he
sent it to the maiden. Delighted at this she
thought, "Prince Siddartha has fallen in love with
me and has sent me a present." The "most noteworthy" parallel, which Professor Seydel says is
introduced by St. Luke into his narrative in such
a way as to show that it is only an awkward
adaptation of the Eastern story, is found in the
words, "And it came to pass, as He said these
things, a certain woman out of the multitude lifted
up her voice and said unto Him, Blessed is the

---

[1] Seydel, *Die Buddha-Legende und Das Leben Jesu nach Den
Evangelien,* "Eine mir neu aufgestossene, höchst merkwürdige
Parallele will ich hier einschalten," p. 20

womb that bare Thee and the breasts which Thou didst suck.   But He said, Yea rather, blessed are they that hear the word of God, and keep it.'[1]

When Gautama was endeavouring to solve the problems of human destiny he sat under a tree, said to be a species of fig-tree. This, Professor Seydel says, is the origin of the incident in the Gospel of St. John, which relates that Our Lord saw Nathanael under a fig-tree. It could scarcely be supposed that criticism, which professes to be serious, could advance any parallelism more extravagant than what I have just quoted. It will then scarcely be credited that Professor Seydel calls attention to the phrase " At that time," as a mode of introducing a new narrative as apparently a reminiscence on the part of the Evangelists of a usage in the Buddhist Books.[2] On such lines it would be possible to disprove the originality of any book or any system the world has ever seen.

Real similarities —not to speak of absurdly far-fetched coincidences —do not, of necessity, warrant the theory of direct relationship. It will always happen in the development of human thought that sometimes the same idea will suggest itself, independently, to different minds. When earnest hearts are pondering over the problems of human life and destiny, and seeking for a solution of the

[1] St. Luke xi. 27, 28.
[2] " Der häufige Uebergang ' Zu dieser Zeit,' um eine ganz neue Erzählung zu beginnen, erinnert an ähnliche Gewohnheiten unsrer Evangelisten." (*Die Buddha-Legende*, p. 66)

difficulties that present themselves in such a study, it is not surprising if the lines, though very often far apart, should sometimes converge or even touch. And if we believe that the Light Divine is a light that lighteth every man that cometh into the world, we need not wonder if a non-Christian religious system should bear some resemblance to Christianity itself. From internal evidence, it appears to me that no case has been made out for the influence of Buddhism upon primitive Christianity. The alleged parallelisms, though striking, do not suggest inter-communication. In many of their essential doctrines the two systems differ absolutely.

The argument from external evidence is com-plicated by the absence of adequate materials for investigating the matter. That the influence of Buddhism *might* have spread to Palestine previous to the Christian era cannot be denied, but that it did so is a point that it would be very difficult to establish. The indications point rather in an opposite direction. Christian writers, prior to Clement of Alexandria, are absolutely silent on the subject of Buddhism. Clement writes with the meagre and imperfect acquaintanceship that bears evidence that he is dealing with a subject of which he knows very little.

The Essenes, who are sometimes claimed to be Buddhist Jews, have, undoubtedly, in their creed and practices, a kind of resemblance to the great system of the East. But all Ascetic systems have certain features of similarity, and the peculiar tenets of the Essenes seem to belong to the influence of Pythagorean, Platonic, or even Zoroastrian speculations, rather than to the spread of Buddhist ideas in Palestine.[1]

It is far more within the range of probability that influences from Persia should have affected this development of Jewish thought; and there is at least as much akin to the system of Zoroaster in the creed of the Essenes as of resemblance to the doctrines of the Buddhists.[2] The conclusions that appear most probable to my mind from an investigation of the evidence are as follows:

There is no direct proof that Buddhism had spread to the neighbourhood of Palestine prior to the Christian era; the indications derived from prevailing forms of thought supply no trace of its influence; the silence of early Christian writers is inconsistent with the idea that the system was one with which they had been brought in contact; and the internal evidence of the Books of the New Testament furnishes no ground whatever for supposing that Buddhism affected the doctrines or conceptions of primitive Christianity.

There is, however, another aspect of this subject that has to be considered. Some of those who concede the independence of Christianity argue that although the two systems grew up without any connection with each other, nevertheless the similarities between them furnish a kind of

[1] *Encyclopædia Britannica*, Art., *Essenes*.
[2] That is, on the theory that they held non-Jewish doctrines. On all this subject see Appendix II.

evidence that what took place in the development
of one of the two creeds is an illustration of
what we may reasonably expect in the other—
that the development of Buddhist thought
supplies a parallel by which we may judge
how Christian conceptions had their origin. The
argument is applied in this way: It is said
that Gautama was an ordinary human being
—save in so far as he was endowed with the
qualities that fitted him for being a teacher and
leader of men. But that the devotion and veneration of his followers willed something more than
this for him : to express their sense of his greatness and wisdom, and of the effect which his
personality had produced on them, they made use
of language that at first clothed itself in the rich
imagery of poetic imagination, but which became
in time crystallized into dogmatic prose, whereby
he was elevated above the level of ordinary men :
the extent of his renunciation was more and more
magnified : a miraculous birth was subsequently
invented for him : supernatural powers came to be
ascribed to him : every law of nature was made
subject to his control : omniscience and omnipo-
tence were his attributes, and finally worship was
offered to him. We have, it is argued, the precise
parallel to this in the development of Christian
belief. We are not able in this case to trace the
course of the growth of the conceptions, but the
deficiency may be supplied by utilizing the information furnished by the parallel system.

The conclusion is drawn, Jesus of Nazareth was

only an ordinary human being, save in so far as
He also possessed the qualities that fitted Him for
being a teacher and leader of men. He lived a
human life and died a human death. But His
followers in like manner were not content with such
a simple record ; they elevated Him above the level
of human kind—invented for Him a miraculous
birth and a renunciation of a previous heavenly
existence ; they ascribed supernatural powers to
Him, and finally endowed Him with Divine attributes and offered to Him adoration and worship.

This parallelism between the early growth
of the Buddhist and the Christian Creed is
drawn out at length by Prof. Rhys Davids in his
Hibbert Lectures. " When we call to mind," he
writes, " how great was the similarity of the outward conditions under which Christianity and
Buddhism arose, how strikingly analogous in many
respects were the mental qualities of the early Christians to those of the early Buddhists, how closely
the personal feelings of the first Christian disciples
to the Christ resembled those of the first Buddhist
disciples to the Buddha, we are naturally very
strongly interested to learn what was the effect in
the case of early Buddhism of causes which must
also have operated in the history of early Christianity."   He goes on then to show how a twofold
cause moulded Buddhist conceptions—the political
idea of a universal monarch who was to rule as
a King of Righteousness and the •philosophical
speculation of all-perfect Wisdom : and he concludes
with a statement that leaves his meaning beyond

doubt. " When we call to mind the process
through which it has become possible for a Christian poet to sing of the Carpenter's Son :—

> ' His Father's home of light,
>   His rainbow circled throne,
>   He left for earthly night,
>   For wanderings sad and lone,'

we shall be able to read between the lines of these
Buddhist Cakka-Vatti legends, and to recognise
in them not merely empty falsehoods, the offspring
of folly or of fraud, but the only embodiment
possible, under those conditions, of some of the
noblest feelings that have ever moved the world."[1]
There is sufficient plausibility in the parallel to
make it dangerous to unreflecting minds. But a
sober examination of the facts of the case makes it
appear in a very different light from what it is here
represented. Now, if two stories are compared
and pronounced to be closely parallel to each other,
but you find on investigation that whatever similarity exists lies only on the surface, and that all
the main points of the narratives are absolutely
different, you naturally conclude that the alleged
parallelism fails. As I read Prof. Rhys Davids'
words I am strongly reminded of a Scripture illustration that seems to show how far his case
for the parallelism between the origins of Christianity and of Buddhism holds. We are told of two
men, each of whom built a house : there was a
similarity between the two structures, for they were

---

[1] Rhys Davids' *Hibbert Lectures*, pp. 128, 140.

both houses—there was just this difference between them, that one house had a firm foundation
of rock, the other was built upon the sand.   The
argument that Prof. Rhys Davids makes use of
amounts to this.   Two men begin to build : they
each erect a house : the houses look to some extent
like each other : you find in course of time that
one of the two houses has no foundation—or only
a foundation on the shifting sand : therefore it
follows as a necessary consequence that the other
house has no foundation, or only one that is similarly undependable.

No reasonable person would adopt such a conclusion, but I fear there are some who read about
the growth of the Buddhist and the Christian
Creed, and without reflection adopt the opinion
that in this case you may argue from the one to the
other : for many people are much more impressed
with a surface similarity than with facts which lie
at the foundation, and which they have not the
patience to investigate.

Now, surely there can be no adequate theory
as to the origin of Christianity that does not
take account of the great fact of the Resurrection.   Whatever view is held as to the written
records of the New Testament, there is no dis-
pute but that from the first the disciples of
Christ believed that their Master had risen again
from the dead.   On this foundation the Christian
Church was built.   Within less than thirty years
after the occurrence was alleged to have taken
place, St. Paul, in a universally acknowledged

Epistle, gives in detail a list of witnesses—most of them then-living witnesses—to whom the risen Master had appeared. The testimony thus produced derives special weight from the fact that St. Paul had been an unbeliever in Christ and had bitterly persecuted His followers. From being an enemy he had become a preacher of the faith of which he once made havoc; and the fifteenth chapter of his first epistle to the Corinthians is a proof that he calmly and thoughtfully weighed the evidence, so as to be thoroughly convinced that the Resurrection of Christ could be supported by valid proof. Here, however, is a cardinal point in which there is an utter absence of parallelism between Christianity and Buddhism. When Gautama was about to die he told his followers that they need expect to see him no more. He said of himself, " So long as the body remains he will be seen by gods and men : but upon the termination of life, when the body is broken up, gods and men shall not see him."[1]

But further, Prof. Rhys Davids states that the conception which the first Buddhist disciples had of the founder of their Creed very closely resembled that which the early Christians formed of their Master. I believe that so far from this being the case, we have evidence to show that the conceptions absolutely differed in the very point which is most essential in the argument. I must again refer to a point touched on in a former Lecture, namely,

[1] Bramajála Sutta.   Quoted by D'Alwis, Buddhist Nirvâṇa, p. 51.

that in Buddhism the system overshadows the personality of the founder. It was the teaching of Gautama that his followers desired to preserve and to perpetuate : the creed is independent of its originator : the four Sacred Truths, which form the centre of the system, are abstract propositions. Hence, although there is reliable evidence for primitive Buddhism, there is no authentic life of Gautama.

Now even such a careful and generally accurate writer as Oldenburg states that it was thus also in early Christianity. He says, " In those (early Buddhist) times the interest in the life of the Master receded entirely behind the interest attached to his teaching. It was exactly the same in the circles of the early Christian Church, and in the circles of the Socratic schools. Long before people began to commit to writing the life of Jesus in the manner of our Gospels, there was current in the young communities a collection of discourses and sayings of Jesus (λόγια κυριακά) : to this collection was appended just so much precise narrative matter as was necessary to call to mind the occasion when and the external surroundings amid which the several discourses were delivered. This collection of the sayings of Jesus laid no claim to any historical arrangement or sequence whatever, or to any chronological accuracy."[1] Reading such statements as these, most people would conclude that there were known written Christian records anterior in date to our Gospels, and

[1] Oldenburg, *Buddha*, pp. 79, 80, English Translation.

on which they were founded, and that both
the nature and manner of the contents of
these primitive sources could be accurately
described.

It is hardly necessary in speaking here to mention that the whole theory built upon the foundation of the Logia being a collection of the sayings
of our Lord rests upon the idea that Logia and
Logoi are convertible terms. In his " Introduction to the New Testament " the Provost has conclusively shown that this theory cannot be maintained.[1]

And if we turn to the earliest records of
Christianity that are in existence—for example to
the four universally acknowledged Epistles of St.
Paul, we find that whereas they contain no mention of any discourse spoken by our Lord, they do
frequently refer to the facts of His Life. The
earliest Christian Creed is expressed in the words
of St. Paul, " I declare unto you the Gospel which
I preached unto you. . . . . how that Christ died
for our sins according to the Scriptures, and that
He was buried, and that He rose again the third
day according to the Scriptures."[2] The conclusion that follows is the direct opposite of that
alleged by Prof. Rhys Davids. The ideas and
statements of the early Buddhists as to the
founder of their system supply no parallel for the
beliefs and views of the early Christians as to the
Person and Life of Christ: a record of the

[1] See Appendix VII.
[2] 1 Corinthians xv. 3, 4.

Buddha's life was only a late afterthought, whereas from the first the acts of Christ's Life formed the basis of Christian instruction.

I need only briefly refer to the different position which miracles hold in the two systems. I have already mentioned that in the Collection of Discourses there is only one miracle attributed to the Buddha, namely, that of crossing the Ganges without bridge or boat, and that the context furnishes an evidence of how the story originated. Even in the Legends there are statements made in direct discouragement of wonder-working.[1] It is, however, beyond the reach of doubt that from a comparatively early period supernatural powers were ascribed to the Buddha : the whole collection of Birth-stories is founded on the belief that he was able to trace his existence through the whole course of antecedent births. But two characteristics mark the miracles which he is alleged to have worked : they are either idle portents, whereby no one could receive benefit ; or else they are wholly introspective, the outcome of an imagination inordinately developed, and in consequence diseased. In the " Book of the Great Decease " there are described, for example, the different stages of mental abstraction through which Gautama is said to have passed before his death. Having attained the preliminary stages, " he entered into a state of mind in which the infinity of space alone was present : then into that in which

[1] See Spence Hardy, *Manual of Buddhism*, p. 303.

I

the infinity of thought alone was present ; then to that in which nothing at all was specially present: next into a state between consciousness and unconsciousness : and finally into a condition in which consciousness both of sensations and ideas had wholly passed away."[1] A miracle, in the Christian sense of the term, in the sense of a moral sign, is unknown in Buddhism : the wonders, such as they are, stand apart from the creed, which is entirely independent of them : the earliest records of Buddhism contain but little mention of them : they multiply as time goes on, until there is no portent too marvellous to be connected with the various events in Gautama's life.

Set in contrast with this the position of miracles in primitive Christianity, and the absence of any parallelism is made most apparent. The miraculous element enters into our earliest records ; the discourses of our Lord are so inextricably interwoven with the miracles which He wrought, that those who deny the reality of His works must be prepared to give up the authenticity of many of the most wonderful words which He is said to have uttered;[2] the miracles were worked with a Divine economy—an unobtrusive quietness—a most merciful purpose, that mark them out as essentially different from idle wonders and extravagant portents.

I conclude this argument with pointing out the basis on which the Sacred Books of the

[1] Mahâ-Parinibbâna-Sutta vi. 11.
[2] Compare St. John ii. 13—22, v. 1—29, vi. 1—14, 26—59, ix. 1—8, 35—41, xi. 23—44, xiv. 1—12, xv. 20—27.

Buddhists stand as contrasted with the Scriptures of the New Testament. The Buddhist Canon was not reduced to writing until between B.C. 88 and 76, during the reign of Vattagamini. Gautama died B.C. 477, according to Max Müller—between B.C. 420 and 400, according to Rhys Davids. In either case an interval of between four hundred and three hundred years elapsed between his death and the writing of the documents. It is quite true that the absence of reliability, which would result in other cases from such a lapse of time, does not apply in the same measure here. The memory of the Indian made tradition a safer method of transmission of teaching than it would be under different conditions. The formation of the Canon, Max Müller states, took place about B.C. 377. About this, however, there is great uncertainty. There is only one ancient list of the Buddhist Books contained in a rock inscription of King Aṣoka, the date of which is B.C. 249. It only includes a few fragments of the Books accounted Canonical.[1]

[1] The inscription is thus translated by Prof. Kern :—"King Priyadarsin (that is, the humane), of Magadha, greets the Assembly (of clerics), [or, greets the assembly of Magadha], and wishes them welfare and happiness. Ye know, sirs, how great is our reverence and affection for the Triad which is called *Buddha* (the Master), *Faith* and *Assembly*. All that our Lord Buddha has spoken, my Lords, is well spoken : wherefore, sirs, it must indeed be regarded as having indisputable authority, so the true faith shall last long. Thus, my Lords, I honour (?) in the first place these religious works : *Summary of the Discipline : The Supernatural Powers of the Master* (or '*of the Masters*'); *The Terrors of the Future ; The Song of the Hermit : The Sûtra on Asceticism ; The Question of Upatishya ;* and *The Admonition to Râhula concerning Falsehood,* uttered by the Lord Buddha. These religious

Now if we were to suppose that the Muratorian Catalogue was the only ancient list of the New Testament Scriptures, and that it both inserted many books now lost and also made no mention of many books now accounted Canonical, we can readily imagine how strongly it would be urged that we had no sure ground to rest upon for primitive Christianity. This ought to be the case in order to draw a parallel between the Buddhist and the Christian Canon.[1] The Sacred Books of Buddhism are confessedly the growth of a considerable period of time. " The Book of the Great Decease," which appears to me one of the most original of all these writings, is regarded by D'Alwis as containing a good deal of the sentiments of Ānanda rather than of Gautama.[2] I have said enough to show how completely the case stated by Prof. Rhys Davids breaks down upon examination. In every essential feature there is dissimilarity instead of parallelism between the origin of the two systems and the evidence upon which they rest.

There is one point in the argument which I have designedly omitted, namely, that which is founded upon the life and character of our Lord as they

works, sirs, I will that the monks and nuns for the advancement of their good name shall uninterruptedly study and remember, as also the laics of the male and female sex. For this end, my Lords, I cause this to be written, and have made my wish evident." (*Corpus Inscriptionum Indicarum*. Second Bairut Rock Edict.)

[1] See Appendix VI.
[2] *Buddhist Nirvâna*, p. 19.

are depicted for us both in the Gospels and in the New Testament generally. I have omitted it, not from any doubt of its validity, but because there are some subjects too sacred to be dragged into the arena of controversy. Some present-day writers use our Lord's name and criticise His claims without the faintest semblance of reverence, and as if they felt themselves at liberty to find fault with Him, or patronize Him, according as they were disposed. There are, I suppose, not many who would care to insert, even in a novel, the sentence to be found in " Robert Elsmere," to the effect that " the toiler of the world as he matures may be made to love Socrates or Buddha, or Marcus Aurelius. It would seem often as though he could not be made to love Jesus " (p. 477, 14th edition).

But even without going to this length, as absurd as it is untrue, there is much written and said of our Blessed Lord that jars painfully on the ear. Those who regard Him only as Man will say they are justified in speaking of Him as they would of any other. But we may often with perfect right decline to follow their lead. We are sometimes asked to discuss the Person and the Claims of Christ in a spirit of philosophic impartiality— tantamount in this case to a spirit of cold indifference. Those who make the demand fail often to realize what it involves. Who could investigate a charge brought against the character of the one dearest on earth to him with the same unmoved spirit in which he might decide on a similar charge brought against a stranger, no

matter how illustrious the stranger might be ?
And when the Divine Personality and the Divine
Claims of Christ are assailed can we be expected
all at once to divest ourselves of those feelings of
profound veneration and grateful love with which
He ever inspires those who realize that to Him we
owe both every present happiness and every future
hope. I say this much because I cannot bring
myself to institute any comparison between the
character of Gautama, who is for us only a hero
and a teacher of bygone days, and the character of
our Lord Jesus Christ, Who, as we believe, died for
us and rose again, Who is eternally present with
us, and Who loves us with an unspeakable and
everlasting love.

The study of Buddhism is one of intense
interest ; I place it far beyond such a system as
Mohammedanism—because it is the result of the
thoughts of one who had no light, other than the
light of nature and of conscience,—because
Gautama was a nobler, purer, truer man than
Mohammed,—because the moral teaching of Buddhism is much higher than that of the Korân. But
nevertheless it has its terrible defects. There is
an eternal world-wide truth in the cry of the
Psalmist, " My soul is athirst for God, yea
even for the living God." In every prayer
which human lips have ever uttered—in every
sacrifice which human hands have ever offered—in
every service which the human heart has ever
framed we may trace an echo, often faint and

broken, but nevertheless an echo of that cry. No system which refuses to recognize the reality and intensity of the cry can satisfy man's deepest need, his need of God Himself. While, therefore, we admire and rightly admire much that we find in Buddhism, the life of its founder—its high morality —the beauty of its sacred literature—neverthe- less, we find in it no substitute for what we believe and hold. " Be ye a refuge unto yourselves," thus Gautama instructed his followers : a truer and a nobler voice makes answer " God is our refuge and strength." " I follow the Buddha, the Law and the Assembly as my guides," so spake the appli- cant for admission to Gautama's Order. A brighter and a higher Creed finds expression in the words, " I believe in God the Father Almighty— in Jesus Christ, His only Son, our Lord—in God the Holy Ghost, the Lord, and Giver of Life."

APPENDIX I.

THE STORY OF BARLAAM AND JOASAPH.

IN the article on " Barlaam " in Smith's Dictionary of Christian Biography, it is stated that "the arguments for the authenticity of this narrative are weak, and it bears internal evidence of being unhistorical. It is attributed to John Damascene, but even this is uncertain." The writer of the article seems to regard the historical character of the story and its authenticity as standing on much the same level of improbability. But whereas it is certain that the story is not historical, the arguments in favour of its authorship are very strong. The difficulty has arisen from the fact that in the title the author is simply described as " John the Monk." Some have supposed that this title designates not John of Damascus, but John of Sinai (fl. circ. A.D. 564). It has, however, been pointed out that the title "John the Monk" is given to St. John of Damascus in some of his undisputed works; that the story of Barlaam and Josaphat[1] contains frequent quotations from Basil and Gregory of Nazianzen, his favourite authors; and that it includes copious extracts from his other writings, notably that " On the Orthodox Faith." [See the preface to the Latin translation, by Billius, of the story of Barlaam and Josaphat.]

What Billius says on the subject of the authorship is more convincing than his remark on the historical character of the narrative; he says that he would

---

[1] This is the form of the name in the Latin translation.

have been more disposed himself to regard it as a religious romance, were it not for the statement of the author that he received it from men incapable of falsehood; "to doubt this," he adds, "would be to place more reliance upon one's own suspicions than upon that Christian charity which thinketh no evil."

On the whole, there seems to be a strong preponderance of evidence in favour of John of Damascus as the author of the story. The circumstances of his life in part help us to understand how he came to write it. It has many points of interest, and as it is not accessible to English readers I give a condensed translation of it. I have omitted the long dissertations on Christian dogmas, except when they touch on the special point of interest, namely, the parallelisms which the author perceived to exist between Christian and Buddhist teaching. I have given all the illustrations; it will appear very evident that some of them are used for a purpose different from what they were originally intended to serve.

A PROFITABLE STORY BROUGHT TO THE HOLY CITY FROM THE FARTHER PART OF ETHIOPIA, CALLED INDIA, BY JOHN THE MONK, AN HONOURABLE AND VIRTUOUS MAN, OF THE MONASTERY OF ST. SABAS, CONTAINING THE LIFE OF BARLAAM AND JOASAPH, FAMOUS AND BLESSED MEN.

Having regard to the danger incurred by the servant who, when he had received the talent from his master, hid it in the earth, I cannot keep silence concerning a useful story which has come to my knowledge, and which pious men from the distant district of Ethiopia, called

India, told me had been translated from trustworthy records. Now the story is as follows: The country of the Indians, which is large and populous, lies far away from Egypt. It is surrounded by seas and navigable bays on the side that looks towards Egypt: it extends inland to the borders of Persia. For a long time it was clouded over by the darkness of idolatry. But when the only begotten Son of God sent forth His disciples to preach to all the nations, the most holy Thomas, one of the twelve, came to India to proclaim the message of salvation. The Lord worked with him and confirmed the word by signs that followed, so that superstition was driven away, and the people adopted the true faith.

When monasteries began to be erected in Egypt, and a number of monks were gathered together in them, the rumour of their virtues and their angelic mode of life spread everywhere; it reached the Indians and stirred them up to like zeal. Many of them left all that they had; they entered into the desert; in their mortal body they adopted the life of the immortals, and many of them, it is said, with golden wings mounted up to heaven.

At this time there arose in that country a king named Abenner: he was wealthy, powerful, victorious over his enemies, and dauntless in war. He was admired both for the size of his stature and the beauty of his countenance; he gloried in his earthly and transient prosperity, in his soul he was the victim of poverty and many evils, for he shared in the folly of the Greeks, in that he was terribly deceived by superstition and idolatry.

He lived in great luxury, and in the enjoyment of the delights and pleasures of life, denying himself the gratification of none of his desires. One cause, however interfered with his happiness and occasioned him much trouble, namely, that he was childless.

The Christians and monks regarded the King's Majesty as of no account ; they feared not his threats, but devoted themselves to those things that pertained to the service of God. They treated as contemptible every earthly delight ; they thirsted after death for Christ's sake, and yearned for the blessedness of martyrdom, and so without fear or reserve they proclaimed the name of God the Saviour. They spake of nothing save of Christ. They clearly taught all men how changeful and impermanent were all things present ; how sure and incorruptible was the life to come. Hence many were rescued from the darkness of deceit, and walked in the pleasant light of the truth ; even some notable persons, members of the royal council, renounced all the burdens of life and became monks.

When the King heard this he was filled with fury ; and he promulgated a decree that all Christians should be compelled to renounce their religion. He sent letters through all the country subject to his rule, to his magistrates and governors bidding them inflict punishment and death upon the righteous. He was specially incensed against the leaders of the monastic order, and waged against them a truceless and remorseless warfare. Many of the faithful wavered in mind ; others who could not endure the torture submitted to the impious proclamation. But the chief monks either endured martyrdom or else hid themselves in desert places and in mountains, not through fear of the threatened torments, but with a holier purpose in view.

At this time one of the King's servants, a chief ruler in rank, who excelled all the rest in valour, in stature,

in beauty, and in every other characteristic that pertains
either to comeliness of person or nobility of mind, having
heard the impious decree, bade farewell to the vain and
degrading pomp and glory in which he had lived; he
resorted to the monks and exiled himself in solitary
places. With noble purpose he purified his senses by
fasting and watching, and by the diligent study of the
sacred Oracles; and having delivered his soul from
every kind of emotion, he shone with the light of dis-
passionate calm.[1]

The King loved him dearly and regarded him as
worthy of every honour. When therefore he heard
that he had embraced Christianity, he was grieved
at the loss of his friend and was more than
ever incensed against the monks. He sought
everywhere for him, and left no stone unturned,
as the saying is, to find him. He was at length
discovered in the desert, and brought before the
tribunal of the King. When he saw him in such
poverty—clothed in rude raiment who had before been
gorgeously apparelled—wasted by a severe, ascetic life
who before had lived in luxury—bearing the evident
traces of being a hermit, he was filled with grief and
anger, and under the influence of both these emotions,
he cried out to him, " O you foolish and senseless man,
wherefore do you choose shame for honour and this
unsightliness for your former glory ? you who were

---

[1] The phraseology is so remarkable and so deeply tinged
with Buddhist conceptions that I give the Greek of the passage.
χαίρειν ειπὼν τῇ ματάιᾳ ταύτῃ καὶ κάτω συρομένη δόξῃ τε
καὶ τρυφῇ, ταῖς τῶν μοναχῶν λογάσιν ἑαυτὸν ἐγκατέμιξεν,
ὑπερόριος γενόμενος ἐν ἐρήμοις τόποις, νηστείαις τε καὶ ἀγρυπνίαις
καὶ τῇ τῶν θείων λογίων ἐπιμελεῖ μελέτῃ τάς αἰσθήσεις ἄριστα
ἐκκαθάρας, καὶ τὴν ψυχὴν, πάσης ἀπαλλάξας ἐμπαθοῦς
σχέσεως, τῷ τῆς ἀπαθείας φωτὶ κατελάμπρυνεν.

president of my kingdom, and chief ruler in my dominions—you have made yourself a laughing-stock to
children. You have not only forgotten our friendship
and happy intercourse, you have gone counter to nature
itself. Your own children you pity not. Wealth and
worldly pomp you regard as of nothing worth, pre-
ferring this dishonour to the honour which encompassed
you. What is it for? What will you gain from honour-
ing Him who is called Jesus before all gods and men, and
from choosing this hard and poverty-stricken existence,
rather than the joys and pleasures of a most happy life?"

When the man of God heard these things he
answered cheerfully and calmly, " If you desire, O King,
to enter into conversation with me, remove, I pray you,
your enemies out of the court, and then I will answer
you." " And who are these enemies," the King said,
"whom you bid me remove?" " Anger and lust," the
holy man answered, "for from the first the Creator
intended them to be fellow-workers with our nature,
and so they are to those who walk not after the flesh
but after the Spirit. But in you, who are altogether
carnal and who have not the Spirit, they are enemies
and opponents. In you lust, when it is gratified, excites
pleasure, but when it is baffled, it causes anger. This
day therefore remove these hindrances, and let prudence
and righteousness preside in their stead, and hear and
judge what I say."

When the King had given his consent, the
hermit said, " If first of all you ask why I
despise what is temporal and give myself wholly to
what is eternal, hearken. Long ago, while I was still
very young, I heard a good and wholesome word: its
power completely possessed me: like a divinely im-
planted seed the remembrance of it sprang up within

my heart : it blossomed and bore the fruit which you
now behold. And this was the scope of that word,
'Fools,' it said, 'despise things that are, as though
they are not ; they lay hold on and interest themselves
in things that are not, as though they are. He who
has not tasted the sweetness of things that are, cannot
learn the nature of things that are not. And not learning, how shall he despise them ? ' And it called what is
eternal and unchangeable 'things that are ' : but the
life present, luxury and pleasure falsely so called, it described as ' things that are not.' To which things, alas !
O King, your heart is enchained. I once was enamoured
of these things, but the force of this saying continually
pierced my soul. My mind which guided me impelled
me to choose the better course ; but the law of sin,
which warred against the law of my mind, bound me,
as it were, with fetters of iron, and held me captive by
the attractive power of things present.

"But, when the kindness and goodness of God our
Saviour delivered me from this terrible bondage, He
strengthened my mind to overcome the law of sin, and He
opened my eyes to discern the evil and the good. Then,
indeed, I perceived that all things present were vanity and
a striving after wind (ματαιότης καὶ προαίρεσις πνεύματος),
as Solomon, the wisest of men, says somewhere in
his writings. Then the veil of sin was taken from
my heart; the darkness that hung over my soul,
arising from the burden of the flesh, was dissipated.
I recognised wherefore I was created, and that I
must ascend to the Creator through keeping of
His commandments. Hence forsaking all things I
followed Him; and I thank God through Jesus Christ
our Lord that He delivered me 'from mortar and brick,'
(ἐρύσατό με τὸν πηλοῦ καὶ τῆς πλινθείας. Exod. i. 14) and

from the cruel and deadly prince of the darkness
of this world ; and that He showed me the short and
easy way whereby in this body of clay I can embrace the
angelic life.   In the desire to attain thereto I choose to
tread the narrow and straitened way, to despise utterly
the vain things of time, and their changeful turnings
and returnings (τῆς ἀστάτου φορᾶς τούτων καὶ περιφορᾶς) :
I am determined to call nothing good, save that which
is good indeed.   From which you, O King, have un-
happily severed yourself.   This is why we are severed
from you ; you are rushing on to sure and certain ruin,
and you would have us be borne along to the like danger.

"So far as the question of earthly service was concerned
we left no part of our duty undone ; you will yourself
bear me witness that I never was charged with indo-
lence nor carelessness.   But when you sought to rob
us of our chief good, namely, our religion, and to make
us wrong God, the worst of all wrongs, and to this end
remind us of honours and benefits, how shall I not say
that you show your ignorance of what is good, when
you set the one against the other, I mean God, and
human friendship with its fleeting glory.   How could
we for such things cast in our lot with you, and not
rather renounce friendship and honour, our affection for
our children, and all else whatever it may be ?   Know
then that I at least will not obey you ; I will not share in
your ingratitude towards God ; I will not deny my Bene-
factor and Saviour, even if you cast me to the wild beasts,
or kill me by sword or fire, things which certainly you
can do.   I fear not death ; I desire not things present ;
I despise their frailty and vanity : which of them is
useful or permanent or satisfying ?   Not only so, but
where they are, there come with them much
wretchedness, much sorrow, much and ceaseless

anxiety. With the pleasure and enjoyment they afford is bound up every trouble and pain ; their riches is poverty ; their glory, ignominy. Who can count the evils they bring with them ?   My inspired teacher tells me briefly, for he says ' *the whole world lieth in evil*,' [1] and ' *love not the world, neither the things that are in the world, for all that is in the world is the lust of the flesh and the lust of the eyes, and the vain glory of life*,' and ' *the world passeth away and the lust thereof, but he that doeth the will of God abideth for ever*.'   Seeking then the good will of God, I forsook all ; I joined myself to those who are possessed by the same desire and seek the same God ; amongst whom there is neither strife nor envy, neither griefs nor cares, but all run the same course that they may obtain the eternal mansions which the Father of Lights prepared for those who love Him.   These men are my parents, my brethren, my friends and intimates.   I have fled far away from my former friends and brethren and dwell in the wilderness waiting upon God who saves me from stormy wind and tempest." [2]

As the man of God cheerfully spoke these apt words the King was moved with anger : he desired to punish the saint severely, but he hesitated and delayed through respect for his dignity and reputation.   At length interrupting him he cried, " Wretched man, you are altogether bent upon your own destruction—driven thereto it would seem by fate ; thy mind and thy

---

[1] This translation of ἐν τῷ πονηρῷ suits the context here far better than the Revised Version rendering," *In the evil one*."

[2] I have thought it well to give this speech nearly in full, because of the ingenious manner in which Buddhist and Christian conceptions are interwoven.

tongue thou hast whetted, and so thou hast poured forth
this foolish and vain talk. Had I not at the beginning
promised to send forth anger out of the council chamber
I would deliver thy body to the fire. But since you
cautiously bound me fast by these terms, I pass over
your temerity on account of our former friendship.
Go then, get out of my sight, I will no longer look on
you, lest I bring you to a terrible end."

The man of God departed into the desert, grieved that
he had not suffered martyrdom. And the King in his anger
stirred up a still fiercer persecution against the monks.

At this time there was born to him a beautiful son,
one who by his comeliness gave proof of what his future
would be. It was said that never in that country had
so graceful and beautiful a child been seen. The King
was filled with the greatest joy at his birth ; he named
him Joasaph ; and he sent about everywhere to gather
crowds to celebrate his birthday. He made a feast for
his people and made presents to his counsellors and
officials, to his soldiers and to those who belonged to
the humbler classes. At that feast upon the boy's birthday there assembled fifty-five chosen men who had
become conversant with Chaldæan astrology. The King
confidentially consulted them and asked each of them
in turn what would be the future of the child who had
been born. After considering for a long time they said
that he would be renowned for his wealth and power
and that he would surpass all who had reigned before
him. But one of the astrologers, who excelled the others,
spake thus : " As I interpret the course of the stars,
O King, the future glory of thy child lies not in thy
kingdom, but in another kingdom greater and incomparably more excellent than thine. For I think that he
will embrace the Christian religion which you persecute,

K

and that no effort will divert him from his aim nor rob him of his hope." When the astrologer spake thus, like Balaam of old, it was not his astrology that enabled him to foretell the truth, but God who, through His enemies, brought the truth to light, so as to leave this ungodly people without excuse. The King was greatly troubled by these words, so that grief cut short his joy. However, in his own city he erected a beautiful palace, and he had magnificent houses constructed in which the boy was to dwell.

As soon as his infancy was passed, he gave orders that he should be kept apart from the world ; he appointed tutors and attendants, young in years and comely in person, who were directed to prevent him from becoming acquainted with any of the miseries of life ; he was to know nothing about death, nor old age, nor sickness, nor poverty, nor aught else that could cause grief or interrupt enjoyment. They were bidden to keep before him everything that was pleasant and delightsome, so that as his mind was enticed and enervated thereby he might lack the power of thinking on the future ; he was above all to hear not one word concerning Christ and His doctrines. The King was specially anxious about this on account of the prophecy of the astrologer. He gave orders that if any of the boy's attendants fell sick, he should be removed with all speed, and another who was hale and hearty substituted in his place, so that his eyes might behold nothing unpleasant. The King planned and did these things, for seeing he did not perceive, and hearing he did not understand.

When he heard that some of the monks still lived (of whom he thought no vestige remained) he was filled with anger, and he sent heralds through the city and the country round about to proclaim that within three days every member of the monastic order was to be banished, and that if any of them were found after the specified days they should be burned alive. For these, he said, are they who persuade the people to worship as their God Him who was crucified.

Meanwhile something happened which affected the King very deeply and made him more than ever enraged against the monks. There was a man who as his prime minister lived in the palace ; he was kind-hearted and pious, seeking as far as possible his own salvation, but secretly, for fear of the King. Some persons, who envied him his intimacy with the King, conspired to accuse him falsely and were constantly looking for an opportunity of carrying out their plan. On one occasion when the King went out to hunt with his usual retinue, this good man was one of those who went out with him. As he was walking along it happened, by Divine Providence I believe, that he met a man in a thicket lying on the ground, whose foot had been terribly crushed by a wild beast. Seeing him passing, the man besought him not to disregard him, but to have compassion on his misfortunes and to carry him to his house. "And," he added, " I shall not show myself unmindful nor ungrateful." The noble man answered, " For the sake of what is right I will help you and give you what care I can ; but what is the benefit which you say I shall receive from you ? " " I am a healer of slander," the poor, weak man replied, " if therefore at any time you should be injured by slander or gossip, I shall cure it with suitable remedies so that it will do you no further harm." He regarded what he said as meaning nothing, but on account of the commandment he determined to bring him to his house, where he took every care of him.

Now those envious men I have spoken of brought to
light the evil of which they had long been in travail. They
falsely accused the prime minister to the King, as being
not only forgetful of his friendship by having renounced
the gods and embraced Christianity, but also as plot-
ting terrible things against the kingdom, perverting the
people and drawing them away after himself. " And if
you wish," they said, " to be assured that we speak the
truth, consult him privately, so as to test him ; tell
him that you wish to forsake the religion of your fathers
and the glory of your kingdom, and to embrace the
monastic life, which you formerly persecuted, as though
you were sorry for what you had done." The King
knew well how great was the fidelity of this man towards
him ; he regarded these statements as incredible and
false, and he determined not to accept them without
proof. So he called him apart and said to him, " You
know, my friend, my feelings towards those who
are called monks and towards all the Christians ; now,
however, I have changed my mind ; I shall treat with
contempt things present, so that I may be partaker of
the hopes of which I have heard them speak, and inherit the eternal kingdom in the life to come, for my
present reign will undoubtedly be cut short by death.
I see no other way of accomplishing my purpose than
that I should become a Christian and renounce the glory
of my kingdom and the delights and pleasures of life ; I
shall seek the ascetics and monks wherever they are,
whom I unjustly persecuted, and cast in my lot with them.
Now what say you to this ? How do you counsel me ?
Speak like truth itself ; for I know that you are sincere
and right-minded above all men." The good man, as
he listened, failed utterly to perceive the snare that was
laid for him : he was touched to the heart, and with

tears he said, " O King, live for ever; it is a good and
wholesome plan you have devised; for though the
kingdom of heaven is hard to find, we must seek it with
all our might; for He says, ' He who seeks it shall find
it ? ' Now the enjoyment of things present, though
apparently productive of pleasure and delight, it is
nevertheless well to renounce; for there is no
reality in it, and those whom it gratifies, it afterwards
tortures sevenfold. Its pleasures and its pains are
less substantial than a shadow; they pass away
more swiftly than the track of a ship that goes over
the sea, or of a bird that flies through the air. The
hope of things to come of which the Christians
speak is sure and steadfast; but it involves affliction in
the world. Our present pleasures are shortlived, and
hereafter there is nothing save punishment to expect
and eternal torment that can never end: the pleasure
is temporal, the pain eternal. But for Christians, the toil
is temporal, the happiness and the profit everlasting.
May the King's good counsel then be accomplished;
for it is well to receive what is eternal in exchange for
what is corruptible."

The King was very indignant as he heard
these words, but he restrained his anger and
said nothing to the man. He however was intelligent and sharp-witted, and he saw that the King was
displeased with him and that he must be the victim of
some plot. He returned to his home pained in heart,
not knowing how to appease the King, and to escape the
danger that threatened him. As he lay awake all the
night long. there came to his mind the recollection of
the man whose foot had been crushed. He summoned
him and said, " I remember that you told me you were
a healer of hurtful words." He answered, " Yes, and if

you wish I shall give you a proof of my skill." The
minister told him of the former goodwill of the
King for him and of their intimacy. He then narrated
his recent crafty consultation with him and how he had
freely made answer to his enquiry; but that the King
had received his advice badly, and that he could tell
by his changed expression what anger lurked in his
breast.

That poor, infirm man thought over the matter, and
said, "Be it known to you, honourable sir, that the
King harbours a suspicion against you, that you want to
seize his realms, and what he said was intended to test
you. Go then, shave your head, put off your gorgeous
apparel, put on garments of hair, and in the morning
enter the King's presence. When he asks you the
meaning of this conduct, answer, " As to what you
enquired of me yesterday, O King, here I am ready to
follow you upon the way that you take. For, though
luxury be enticing and pleasant, far be it from me to
cling to it when you have renounced it. Though the
path of virtue be rough and difficult, with you it will be
easy, smooth, and pleasant. As you made me partaker
of the pleasures here, so will you find me join in what
is painful, that I may share with you in what is to come.'

The noble man took the advice of his humble friend,
and did as he bade him. And when the King saw and
heard him, he was delighted, perceiving with joy his
loyalty to him. He knew now that what had been
alleged against him was false, and he made him
recipient of greater honour and more intimate friendship than ever. But against the monks his anger was
intensified, for he said that this was their teaching,
that men should renounce pleasure, and be deluded
with false hopes, like as with dreams.

Now the King's son, of whom I have spoken, was kept apart in the palace that had been erected for him: he was now a youth, and had gone through the whole course of study prescribed by the Ethiopians and Persians: he was noble in person and prudent in heart, and conspicuous in every virtuous accomplishment. He propounded questions concerning nature to his teachers, which made them marvel at his quickness and intelligence. The King was charmed with the grace of his countenance and the culture of his mind: he kept telling those who were attending on the boy to allow none of the painful aspects of life to become known to him: not a word was to be said about death interrupting present enjoyment. But he buoyed himself up with vain hopes, and he was like one shooting arrows to try and hit the sky, as the proverb goes; for how could death escape the notice of any human being? And truly it escaped not the notice of the boy. For, since his reason and intellect were fully developed, he considered with himself why his father kept him apart and would not allow anyone who pleased to come to him; for he knew well that this must be his father's command. Nevertheless, he feared to ask him, for it seemed to him incredible that his father should not do what was for his good; and, further, he thought that if the thing was done by his father's will, and if he should ask about it, that he should not find out the truth. So he determined to ask others rather than his father. Now he had one tutor who was of all most dear and most intimate with him; he treated him with special kindliness and made him splendid presents, and then he asked him why the King kept him confined within the palace grounds. "And," he added, "if you give me a truthful

answer, I will make a compact of perpetual friendship
with you." The tutor was a man of understanding
himself and knowing the cleverness and thoughtfulness
of the youth, lest he should involve himself in danger,
he told him everything; the persecution carried on by
the King against the Christians, specially the ascetics;
how they were driven away and banished; and what
the astrologers had predicted concerning him at his
birth. "In order, then," he said, "that you may not
hear their doctrines, nor incline to their religion, the King
takes care that only a chosen few should be admitted to
your presence; and he has given us orders to let you
know nothing of the dark side of life."

When the boy heard this he said nothing;
but a good impression was made upon him; the
grace of the Comforter began to open the eyes of
his understanding, leading him to the true God, as
the story will go on to show. For as the King came often
to see him, since he loved the boy, on one occasion he
said to him, "I want to know something from you, my
lord and king, on account of which my soul is consumed
with grief and care." The father felt his heart turn
cold at this and he said, "Tell me, dearest child, what is
the trouble that disturbs you, and I shall try to turn it
into joy." The boy said, "Why am I kept here, shut up
within these walls and gates? why am I secluded from
the society of men?" The King answered, "I do not
wish, my child, that you should see anything that would
pain your heart and interfere with your enjoyment; I
desire that you should pass your entire life in ease with
pleasures and delights surrounding you." "But, my
lord," the boy said, "in this fashion I do not live in joy
and happiness, but rather in affliction and distress, so
that my very meat and drink are distasteful to me. I

long to see what lies outside these gates.   If you wish,
then, that I should not live in pain, let me go forth and
delight myself by seeing what has been kept secret from
me."   The King was troubled, but he thought that if he
refused his request, he would cause him still more pain.
So he ordered horses and a royal retinue to be ready
to accompany him when he wished to go forth.   But he
ordered his attendants to keep everything unpleasant
from his eyes; to show him only what was beautiful and
delightsome: and he directed companies of musicians
to go down the streets singing sweet songs and acting
pleasant plays to divert and please his mind.

Thus the King's son went frequently out; but it
once happened, through the carelessness of his attendants, that he saw two men—one of them leprous, the
other blind.   When he saw them he was troubled, and
he said to those who were with him, "Who are these?
What is this terrible sight?"   Since they could not conceal what he had now seen, they said, "These are human
misfortunes which afflict mortals when the material
body becomes diseased."   The youth said, "Do these
things happen to all?"   "Not to all," they replied,
"but to those whose health is injured by noxious
humours."   Again he asked, "Well, if these things do
not happen to all, do those to whom they are destined
to come know beforehand of them? or do they come
at haphazard and without warning?"   "What man,"
they answered, "can see and know the future?   This
is more than human nature can attain to: it is the
prerogative of the gods."   The Prince ceased his
questions, for he was grieved to the heart by what
he had seen; and the expression of his face was
changed by the strange occurrence.

Not many days after he went forth again and met

an old man with wrinkled face and palsied limbs, bowed down and white-headed, toothless, and with a faltering voice. Astonishment seized the Prince; he asked that he might be brought near to him, and once again enquired the meaning of this strange sight. Those who were with him said, " He has lived out his life; his strength is gradually failing; his limbs are feeble; and he has thus come to that wretched plight in which you see him." " And what," he asked, " will the end be?" They answered, " Death alone awaits him." " But is this the destined lot of all men, or does it happen only to some?" " Unless death prematurely carries a man off, it is impossible as time goes on that he should escape this experience." Then the youth said, " After how many years does this happen to a man? And is death absolutely necessary? Is there no means of escape and of deliverance from this misery?" They answered, " Men arrive at old age in eighty or one hundred years; then they die: it cannot be otherwise: death is a debt to nature, imposed on man from the first, and its approach is inevitable." When the intelligent and thoughtful youth heard this he groaned from the depths of his heart, and said, " Bitter indeed is this life, and full of pain and sorrow of every kind, if these things are so. How can anyone be free from care in prospect of death, whose approach, as you say, is both inevitable and uncertain?" He went away turning these things over in his mind: he thought of them incessantly. Death came often before him, and caused him dejection and sorrow. " For," he said to himself, "when shall death come to me? Who will remember me when I am dead, since time consigns all things to oblivion? When I die shall I be annihilated?

Or is there another life and another world?" As he
continually thought thus, he became pale and worn,
but whenever he met his father he assumed a cheerful
and bright expression, not wishing that he should
know his trouble. But he longed with an irresistible
desire for some one who could satisfy his heart and
speak a word of comfort to him. When the youth was
in this state, yearning in his soul to find what was
good, the Eye that sees all things beheld him, and He
who willeth all men to be saved and to come to the
knowledge of the truth passed him not by, but manifested towards him His wonted kindness, and in this
manner revealed to him the way wherein he should go.

There was at that time a monk, wise in Divine truth,
upright in life and sound in doctrine, one who diligently
practised every ordinance of the monastic life. Whence
he sprang, and to what family he belonged I cannot say;
but he dwelt in a solitary place in the land of Shinar,
and he had attained the dignity of the priestly office.
This aged man's name was Barlaam. By Divine revelation he learned all about the Prince, so that leaving the
desert he returned to inhabited districts. There he
changed his dress and put on gorgeous apparel; he em-
barked on board ship and came to the kingdom of India,
where he assumed the appearance of a merchant and
came to the city where was the palace of the Prince.
There he passed many days making enquiry about
him and his attendants; and when he ascertained that
the tutor of whom I have spoken was most intimate
with him, he came privately to him and said, "I wish
you to know, my lord, that I have come as a merchant
from a distant land, and I have with me a precious
jewel the like of which has never been found. Up to
the present I have told no one of it, but I inform you

about it because I perceive that you are a prudent and
intelligent man, and if you bring me to the Prince, I
shall bestow it upon him. It incomparably surpasses
every treasure. It can give the light of wisdom to those
who are blind in heart ; it can open the ears of the
deaf, give speech to the dumb and health to the sick;
it makes wise the simple ; it drives demons away ; it
supplies to him who possesses it everything good and
pleasant." The tutor replied, " I perceive that you are
a man of a well-balanced mind, but your words seem
extravagantly boastful. For as to precious stones and
pearls, how can I tell you how many of them I have
seen ? But never did I see nor hear of a jewel possessing powers such as you describe. Still, show it to me,
and if it be as you say, I shall speedily bring it to the
Prince, and you will receive in return the greatest
honours and gifts from him. Until I am satisfied by
seeing it myself it is impossible for me to announce this
strange and extravagant story to my master and king."
Barlaam answered, " It is true that you have never seen
nor heard powers and capacities such as this jewel
possesses, for what I speak of is no every-day occurrence, but something strange and marvellous. But as
to your request to see it, listen to what I have to say.
This jewel along with its other powers possesses this
characteristic, that he cannot safely behold it who has
not strong and healthy vision and a body pure and
wholly undefiled. If anyone not possessed of these
two qualifications were to look upon it, he would lose at
once such power of vision and of mind as he possessed.
Now, I am not unskilled in medicine and I perceive that
your eyes are delicate ; I fear therefore lest I should
cause you to lose your sight. I have heard however that
the Prince leads a correct life, that his eyes are strong

and beautiful, so that I do not fear to show the stone to
him. Do not therefore hesitate to tell him about it, lest
haply you deprive your master of this treasure." He
answered, " If these things are so, do not show me the
stone. My life has been marred by many sins: my eyes
are not strong, as you see. I shall however be
persuaded by you and I shall tell my lord and king
concerning it."

When the Prince heard the words of his tutor, he was
filled with joy and spiritual gladness, and becoming, as
it were, inspired in soul, he ordered the man to be
brought in at once.

When Barlaam entered his presence he gave him first
of all the usual greeting of peace; and when the tutor
had retired Joasaph said to him, "Show me this precious
jewel about which I have heard that you speak such
strange and wonderful things." Barlaam answered, " I
must say nothing false nor ill-considered to one in your
position ; everything that has been said to you concerning me is accurately true ; but unless I first test
your disposition, I cannot reveal the mystery. For my
Master says, ' *The sower went forth to sow his seed* ' [here
follows the parable]. If then I find in your heart good
and fruitful soil, I shall not hesitate to implant the
divine seed and to reveal the great mystery. But if it
be rocky or thorny or a way trodden by all who will,
it were better not to sow this good seed, than to allow
it to be carried away by the fowls of the air and the
beasts of the earth, before which I am forbidden to cast
pearls. But I am persuaded ' *better things concerning you
and things that accompany salvation*,' that you will both
behold this priceless stone, and that by the brilliancy
of its light you will see light and bear fruit an hundred-
fold. For it was on your account that I determined to

take this long journey that I might show you what you have never seen and teach you what you have not heard."

The Prince then told him of his anxiety to learn the truth, and that it was with this desire that he had at once admitted him to his presence. And Barlaam said, "You acted well and worthily of your royal dignity: you show that your heart is set, not on unreal greatness, but on the hidden hope. Now there was once a great and glorious King, and it came to pass that as he was journeying in a golden chariot with his royal retinue accompanying him, he met two men clad in torn and squalid garments, and with pale, emaciated faces. When the King saw them he alighted from his chariot and falling to the ground he did obeisance to them; then rising up he embraced them and greeted them in a most friendly manner. His courtiers and officers were very indignant, for they thought he was acting unworthily of his royal dignity. But as they did not venture openly to find fault with him, they requested his own brother to speak to the King not thus to put to shame the glory of his sovereign power. When he had complied with their request the King answered him in a way which he did not understand. For the King had a custom when he sentenced any person to death to send a herald to his door with a trumpet, called on this account "the trumpet of death," and by the sound of the trumpet everyone knew that the man had been condemned to die. On that evening the King gave orders that the trumpet of death should sound at his brother's door. When he heard the trumpet sound, he gave up hope and spent the night arranging his affairs. At dawn he clad himself in mourning, and with his wife and children went to the palace weeping and lamenting his fate.

The King admitted him, and when he saw his grief he
said, " O silly and senseless man, if you so dread the
herald of your brother, who is one like yourself, and
whom you know you have never offended, how can you
blame me when I humbly salute the heralds of my God,
who, more clearly than with a trumpet, warn me of
death and the dread approach of my Master, against
whom I know that I have sinned often and deeply ?
Now in order to convince you of your folly I treated
you in this way ; and I intend so also to convince those
who suggested to you to find fault with me." After
this wise instruction he sent him away to his home.
He then ordered four wooden caskets to be made :
two were overlaid with gold ; and having filled them
with dead men's bones, he fastened them with golden
chains. The two others were smeared over with pitch
and tar ; but they were filled with precious stones and
pearls and sweet perfumes ; and these caskets he tied
up with ropes of hair. He then summoned the courtiers
who had found fault with his treatment of those men ;
he placed before them the caskets and asked them to
compute the value of the one set and of the other.
They decided that those that were overlaid with gold
were worth most, " for," they said, " it must be that
kingly crowns and girdles are enclosed in them." But
those that were smeared over with pitch and tar, they
decided were of poor and contemptible value. The
King said to them, " I knew that you would thus decide,
for with your bodily eyes you judge only what your eyes
behold. Thus it should not be, it is with the eyes of the
understanding you should decide what is precious and
what is worthless." He ordered them then to open the
gold-plated caskets, and when they were opened a foul
smell and sight met them. The King said, " This is the

type of those who array themselves in rich and sump-
tuous dress, and pride themselves upon their pomp
and glory; but within they are full of deadly things and
of evil works." Then, having ordered the caskets smeared
with tar to be opened, all who were present were
delighted with the beauty and sweet perfume of what
they contained, And he said to them, " Know ye to
whom these are like ? They are like those humble
and illclad men whose outer appearance, when you
beheld it, you deemed it a wrong that I should bow
down on the ground before them; but with the eyes of
my understanding I perceived their worth and dignity;
through contact with them I was honoured, for I deem
them worthy of greater respect than any royal crown
or purple robe." Thus he put them to shame, and he
taught them not to be misled by mere externals, but to
take heed to realities. As did then that wise and pious
King, so have you done in admitting me, for the sake
of that good hope, of which I do not think you will be
disappointed." Joasaph said to him, " Your words are
good and apt, but this I want to know, Who is your
Master, who at the beginning of your speech you said
had taught you about the seed ? "

[Here follows a long description by Barlaam of the
Creation, the Fall, the progress of idolatry, the call
of Abraham, the history of the Jews, the Incarnation,
the Life, Death, Resurrection and Ascension of our
Lord, and the formation of the Christian Church.]

When the King's son heard these words, light
entered his soul: he rose from his throne in joy, he
embraced Barlaam and said to him, " Perchance, most
honourable man, this is that priceless jewel which,
naturally, you shrouded in mystery, not showing it to
everyone who wishes, but to those who are strong in

spiritual discernment. For lo! as I received these
words with my ear, light most pleasant entered into
my heart, and that heavy cloud of grief that has over-
hung me so long was all at once dispersed. Tell me if I
am right, and if you know anything better than what you
have told me—do not hesitate to declare it unto me."

[Barlaam is thus led to speak of admission into the
Christian Church by baptism, and of the hope of
eternal life in the kingdom of heaven. He treats at
great length of the Resurrection. It is impossible not
to feel in this section of the treatise that the author is
consciously meeting the views of those who regarded
Nirvána as the consummation most to be desired, and
that he is setting before them the path of life as the
more excellent way. In the course of the conversation
Barlaam was led to speak on the folly of idolatry, of
which he gives the following illustration, which it is
manifest was originally intended to serve quite a
different purpose.]

" To what shall I liken those who are guilty of this
folly [of idolatry]. I shall give you an illustration
which was told to me by a very wise man. He said
that idolaters were like a bird-catcher, who having
caught a little bird called a nightingale was about to
kill and eat it. But the nightingale being given the
power of speech said to him, 'What advantage is it for
you to kill me, for with me you cannot satisfy your
hunger ? But if you let me go, I shall give you three
directions, which if you observe you will greatly benefit
your entire life.' The bird-catcher, filled with wonder,
promised that if he heard from the nightingale anything
which he did not already know, he would set it at
liberty. Then turning towards the man it said, ' Never
attempt what you cannot perform : Never regret a thing

L

that is past: Never believe an incredible story. Observe
these three precepts, so that it may be well with you.'
The bird-catcher was pleased with the good sense of the
directions and he let the bird go free. Now the
nightingale wished to know if the man had com-
prehended the meaning of the words, and would reap
benefit from them, and so it tested him thus. It flew
towards him and cried, 'O foolish man that you are!
what a treasure you have lost to-day! For I have inside me a pearl larger than the egg of an ostrich.'
When the bird-catcher heard this he was smitten with
deep regret that he had allowed the nightingale to
escape from his hands, and in the desire once more to
get possession of it, he cried, 'Come to my house, where I
shall sumptuously entertain you and let you go free again
after I have paid my respects to you.' Then the nightingale said to him, ' Now I know what a foolish man you
are, for though you gladly heard what I said to you, my
directions have done you no good.   I told you never to
regret a thing that was past, and lo! you are smitten
with grief because I have escaped your hands.   What
is this but regretting the past?   I told you never to
attempt what was impossible, and now you are trying to
catch me, though you cannot follow me in my flight.   I
told you never to believe what was incredible, and yet
you believe that I have inside me a pearl larger than
my body, never pausing to think that I am not myself
as large as an ostrich's egg, and so could not contain a
pearl of that size.' "

Such also is the folly of those who trust in their idols.
They form them with their hands, and worship what their
fingers have made, saying, "Ye are our creators." Yet
how can they suppose that what they have formed,
formed themselves?   They keep their idols in safety,

lest they should be carried off by thieves, yet they call
their idols their protectors.   And they never reflect what
folly it is to suppose that if they are unable to take care
of themselves, they can take care of others.   *"For why,"*
saith He, *"do they resort to the dead on behalf of the
living?"*

[This leads on to an earnest exhortation to Joasaph to
flee from idolatry, which he professes himself ready to
renounce.   He makes inquiry, then, concerning the life
which he is to lead after he has been baptized.   Barlaam
instructs him in Christian duties, and in the course of
his description of the life appointed for the disciples of
Christ, he is led to speak of the asceticism of the monks.
The section is interesting because of the points of contact
with the rules laid down for the members of Gautama's
Order of Mendicants.]

"Some spend their life in the open air, exposed to the
burning heat of the sun, to bitter cold, to rain and storm.
Others construct huts for themselves, or live hidden
away in caves and dens of the earth.   So eager are they
in the pursuit of virtue, that they utterly renounce every
carnal comfort and refreshment ; their food consists of
herbs, and vegetables, and fruits, or else of dry and very
hard bread ; and they not only bring their excessive
abstinence to bear upon the quality of their food, but
they reduce its quantity also to the smallest dimensions,
eating only barely enough to keep themselves alive.
Some fast all the week, and eat only on Sunday ; others
eat twice in the week ; others merely taste food once every
day.   In prayer and watching they fall but little short of
the very Angels ; they have as absolutely renounced
silver and gold, buying and selling, as though such things
did not exist.   Living as exiles, and mindful always of
death, gentle, forbearing and silent, poor and destitute,

humble and peaceful, in perfect charity with God and
man, they pass their life here as if they had the disposition of the Angels. Hence God endued them with the
power of working wonders and signs and miracles of
various kinds, and He has caused the fame of their mode
of life to spread to the farthest limits of the world.

"Those, on the other hand, who ceaselessly yield themselves to the enjoyment of carnal pleasures, and allow
their soul to be consumed with hunger and to be weighed
down by countless ills, seem to me to be like a man
fleeing from a mad unicorn ; and who, being terrified
by its fierce bellowing, ran away at full speed lest it
should devour him, and as he ran fell into a deep pit.
He stretched out his hands while falling, and caught
hold of a shrub, which he tightly grasped. He was
able to place his feet upon a kind of step, and he
thought that now he would be in peace and safety.
But as he looked about, he saw two mice, one white and
the other black, gnawing away at the root of the shrub
out of which he hung, and he perceived that they had
almost cut it in two. He looked down then to see how
deep was the pit, and there he beheld a terrible dragon
with fiery breath and fierce eyes, gaping to devour him.
Again he looked at the step upon which his feet rested,
and there he saw the heads of four serpents protruding
from the wall into which it was fastened. But as he
looked up, he saw some honey dropping from the
branches of a tree overhead. And forgetful altogether
of the dangers that threatened him—though the mad
unicorn was without, ready to devour him, and the
terrible dragon beneath, longing to swallow him ; though
the root of the shrub from which he hung suspended was
almost cut through, and his feet were resting on a
slippery and most insecure step ; nevertheless, utterly

forgetful of these dangers, so many and so great—he foolishly became absorbed in the attempt to taste a little of the sweetness of that honey. This is a type of those who are ensnared by the deceits of the life present ; and I shall explain the illustration to you. The unicorn resembles death, which is always pursuing and endeavouring to overtake the sons of Adam ; the pit is the world, which is full of manifold evils and of deadly snares ; the shrub whose root was perpetually being gnawed away by the two mice, is the course of the life of each individual, which is consumed by the hours of night and day, and gradually brought to an end ; the four serpents represent the combination in the human body of the four fluctuating and impermanent elements, by whose disarrangement and disturbance the constitution of the body is destroyed. Moreover, that fierce and fiery dragon resembles hell, which pants to receive those who prefer present delights to future blessings. And the drops of honey represent the sweetness of the pleasures of the world, whereby it deceives those who are its friends, and hinders them from considering their own salvation.

" But, further, those who are enamoured of the pleasures of life and the delights which they afford, and who consequently prefer what is frail and fleeting to that which endures for ever, are like a man who had three friends, two of whom he highly honoured, and to whom he was so greatly attached that he would incur any danger and undergo any toil on their behalf. But the third he treated with great contempt ; he neither conferred any favour upon him nor did he reciprocate his affection, but entertained towards him only a feeling of very slight and surface friendship. Now it happened one day that a band of fierce and violent soldiers came to seize this man, and to bring him with all haste before the king,

because he owed a debt of ten thousand talents. In his
distress, he sought some friend who would help him in
the terrible account which he had to settle before the king.
He went first to the friend with whom he was most intimate, and said to him, 'You know, my friend, how I
exposed my life on your behalf; now I seek your aid in
the time of my own sore trouble. How much will you
lend me? How much may I hope from you who are of
all dearest to me?' He answered him, ' Man, I am no
friend of yours ; I know not who you are. I have other
friends with whom I must enjoy myself to-day ; hence-
forward they shall be my associates. Here are two rags
which you may take for your journey, they will be no
use to you, but do not expect anything else from me.'
When he heard these words, he gave up all hope of help
from him ; and so he went to the second friend, and said
to him, 'You know how I honoured you and helped you;
to-day I am in trouble and misfortune, I pray you help
me. Tell me, therefore, what I may expect from you?'
He answered, 'I have no leisure to-day to attend to you ;
I have troubles, and anxieties, and difficulties of my own.
I will go a little way with you, though that will do you
no good, and then I shall return and devote myself to
my own affairs.' So he came back with empty hands,
utterly at a loss what to do, bemoaning his vain hopes
reposed in his careless and useless friends, who had
made such a base return for his affection towards them.
He went off to the third friend, whom he had scarcely
noticed, and whom he had never invited to participate in
his pleasures, and he said to him, with downcast face, ' I
can scarcely bring myself to speak to you, because I
know very well that you are conscious that I have never
done a good turn to you, nor treated you as a friend ; a
terrible calamity has, however, befallen me ; my other

friends have altogether disregarded my plea, and, though
I am ashamed to do it, I have come to you to see if you
can give me some little help. Do not refuse me, nor
remind me of my bad treatment of you.' With a bright
and happy face he answered, 'Nay, truly you are my
greatest friend ; whatever little kindness you have shown
me I shall repay with interest. Do not be afraid nor
anxious. I shall precede you, and entreat the king on
your behalf ; you shall not be delivered into the hands of
your enemies. Be of good cheer, dearest friend, and
grieve no more.' As he listened, he burst into tears,
and cried, 'Alas ! which shall I lament and bewail first,
my heartless, ungrateful, and false friends, or my own
terrible neglect of you ? You have proved yourself my
true and real friend.'

"Now the first friend represents riches and the lust
for lucre, for which men endure countless perils and
anxieties ; but when the hour of death comes, they
receive in return only the worthless rags requisite for
their funeral. The second friend resembles wife and
children, and the rest of one's kinsfolk and intimates,
to whom we are bound by a tie of affection so hard to
sever, that for their sake we neglect our own soul and
body : and not one of them is of any service to us in
the hour of death, they merely follow our body to the
tomb, and then they immediately return and busy themselves about their own concerns, forgetting us as soon
as they have covered us in the grave. The third friend,
despised and overlooked, whose presence was never
sought, but who was avoided and kept at a distance,
resembles good works, such as faith, hope, love,
bountifulness, kindness, and the other virtues, which go
before us when we leave our bodies, and entreat the
Lord for us, so that we are delivered from our enemies

and those terrible exactors who would bring an awful account against us, and seek to inflict on us a grievous penalty. This is the good and well-disposed friend who bears in mind our few good acts and repays them with interest."

Joasaph expressed himself pleased, and asked an illustration of the vanity of the world, and how we may pass through it in peace and safety.

Barlaam replied, "I have heard of a great city where the custom prevailed of choosing a stranger about whom the citizens knew nothing, and who was absolutely unacquainted with the laws and customs of the city, and appointing him king over them, granting him for the space of a year absolute and unlimited power. Then suddenly while he thought himself quite secure, and was living in luxury and wantonness, supposing that his kingdom would last for ever, they rose up against him, rent off his royal robe, and carried him in a triumphal procession, naked, through the city, then banished him to a distant island, where, without food or clothes, he suffered terribly from hunger and exposure ; and the luxury and mirth he so unexpectedly had enjoyed, were once again changed into an equally unexpected grief and trouble. Now it happened that, in accordance with the custom of that state, there was a man appointed king who was exceedingly intelligent. He was neither carried away by his unlooked-for prosperity, nor did he follow the example of those who went before him, and who had been so cruelly expelled, by living in thoughtless security ; but he was careful and anxious how best to provide for his own interests. He often thought over the matter, and he was informed by a very wise counsellor concerning the custom of the country and the place of perpetual exile, so that he might be on his

guard against it. When he heard this, and ascertained
that soon he would be carried off there, and leave his
kingdom to others, he opened his treasures, to which
he still had free access, and he entrusted to some faithful
servants a great quantity of silver and gold and precious
stones, which they were to convey beforehand to the
island where he was to be exiled. When the appointed
year was over, his citizens rose in rebellion ; they
stripped him and banished him like those who had
been before him. The other *quondam* kings were in
terrible distress ; but he had stored up riches beforehand, so that he lived in ease and luxury, having no fear
of those lawless and wicked citizens, and he con-
gratulated himself upon his happy plan."

[Barlaam expounds the illustration, and Joasaph in-
quires how it is possible to send forward riches to the
world to come, so that they may there be fully and fearlessly enjoyed, Barlaam answered,] "We send forward
wealth by the hand of the poor. For one of the
prophets, the wise Daniel, said to the King of Babylon,
'Wherefore let my counsel please thee, O king, make
redemption for thy sins by almsgiving, and for thy
unrighteousness by showing pity to the poor.' And
the Saviour says, 'Make to yourselves friends with the
mammon of unrighteousnes, that when ye die, they may
receive you into eternal habitations.' And up and
down through the Gospels we learn that our Master
spoke frequently of almsgiving and contributions to the
poor." Then Joasaph asked, "And is this life of self-
renunciation, with all the hardships it involves, an
ancient tradition that has been handed down to you
from the Apostles ? Or is it only a new plan devised by
yourselves, as the more excellent way ?" The old man
answered, "It is no law recently introduced that I

inform you about, God forbid, but what we have received
from old time. Our Lord once bade a rich man sell all
that he had and give to the poor, and He said, 'thou
shalt have treasure in heaven, and come take up the
cross and follow Me.' Wherefore the saints, in all ages,
mindful of His command, are careful to rid themselves
of every difficulty of this kind; they give everything
away, and by distributing to the poor, they store up
wealth for themselves in heaven; they bear the cross,
and follow Christ, some by suffering martyrdom, others
by adopting the ascetic life, and thereby, according to
the teaching of our true philosophy, becoming in no
sense inferior to the martyrs."

Joasaph professed his desire to sever himself from the
vanity of his previous life, and to spend the rest of his
days with Barlaam, so that for the sake of what was
temporal. and impermanent, he might not forfeit what
was eternal and incorruptible.

The old man said, " If you do this, you will act like a
wise youth I have heard of, who was born to rich and
distinguished parents. His father arranged a marriage
for him with the daughter of a friend who was nobly
born and very rich; the lady herself was exceedingly
beautiful; but when his father told the youth what he
had planned for him, he thought it so strange and distasteful that he ran away and left his father. He came
in his flight to the house of a poor old man, where he
desired to rest during the heat of the day. This man
had one only daughter, a maiden; she was sitting just
then at the door working with her hands, but with her
voice she was singing praise to God from the depth of
her heart. As he listened to her Hymn, the youth said,
'What is this you are doing, Lady? How can you who
are so poor offer thanks for great gifts and praise the

Giver of them?' She answered, 'Know you not that a
small dose sometimes frees men from a terrible disease?
In the same way thanking God for small mercies is a
source of great blessing. I am indeed the daughter of
a poor·old man; but I thank God for what He has given
me; knowing that He who has given me so much can
give me greater things than these. Now with regard to
the earthly gifts which we do not possess, those who
have them derive no real benefit from them, nay they
sometimes do them harm; those who are without them
suffer no real injury; if you take into consideration that
journey which all have to take, and the end which awaits
all persons alike. But with regard to what is most
necessary and of real importance, gifts of this kind I
have received in countless number from my Master. I
have been created in the image of God; I have come to
know Him; I have the gift of reason; I have been called
from death to life through the mercy of God; I am
privileged to partake of His mysteries; the gate of
Paradise is opened for me, if I will I can enter, no man
forbidding me. These are gifts bestowed equally on poor
and rich; I know not how to thank God for them; how
should I excuse myself if I stopped singing His praise?'

"The youth was much pleased with her intelligent
words, and calling her father, he said to him, 'Give me
thy daughter, for I am charmed with her good sense and
piety.' But the old man said, 'You cannot take the
daughter of a poor man, for you are well-born.' 'But I
shall take her,' the youth answered, 'unless you refuse
her to me: for the daughter of wealthy parents was
betrothed to me, but I rejected her and ran away. And
now I love your daughter because of her piety towards
God and her intelligence, and I wish to marry her.' The
old man replied, ' I cannot give her to you to carry her

off to your father's house, nor can I separate her from
me, for she is my only child.' 'Then,' said the youth, 'I
shall stay with you, and adopt your way of life,' so he
put off his gorgeous apparel and put on clothes which
the old man gave him. And after he had tried and
tested him in many ways, so as to ascertain whether he
was steadfast in his purpose, and not merely infatuated
by his love for his daughter, but that from motives of
piety he chose a life of poverty rather than his former
pomp and glory, he caught him one day by the hand,
brought him into an inner chamber, and he showed him a
great store of wealth, such as the youth had never before
seen, and he said to him, 'All these things do I give
you ; as you desire to be the husband of my daughter,
the heir to my possessions.' And when he received the
inheritance, he surpassed in riches all the great men of
the earth."

[Barlaam gave Joasaph then some further instruction
in Christian doctrine] and when he had thus spoken he
taught him the Creed drawn up at the Council of Nicæa,
and he baptized him into the Name of the Father, and
of the Son, and of the Holy Ghost, in the pond that was
in his park. The grace of the Holy Spirit came upon
him. Barlaam led him back to his room, where he
celebrated the holy rite of the bloodless sacrifice, and
administered to him the spotless mysteries of Christ,
whereupon he rejoiced in spirit, and gave glory to Christ,
His God.

Meanwhile his tutors and attendants began to remark
the frequent visits of Barlaam to the prince, and one of
them named Zardan at length spoke to Joasaph, and told
him that he was apprehensive as to the consequences
when the king heard what was taking place. The prince
then invited him to conceal himself behind a curtain in

his room, so that he might hear what Barlaam said. Zardan adopted the suggestion, and thus discovered, to his dismay, that Joasaph had embraced the Christian faith. He pleaded with the prince to reflect how his father would be affected when he heard the tidings. Joasaph besought him for the present to say nothing about it to the king.

Just at this time Barlaam informed him that he must return to his own home, and though the prince was stricken with sorrow at the thought of parting from him, nevertheless he so dreaded lest Zardan should give information to the king, that he told him he durst not deter him from going away. He asked him to accept a gift of money from him, but this Barlaam refused. He then begged him to leave with him the old threadbare cloak which he wore, and to allow him to give him a new garment in return. Barlaam consented to give him the cloak, but he said it was unlawful for him to receive a new garment ; he would, however, accept any rough rags of haircloth which the prince could find. He then prayed for him and departed.

After his departure Joasaph gave himself up to a life of prayer ; by day and by night he was constant in his supplications. Zardan became alarmed lest he should do himself some terrible harm by the life which he was leading, and he at length informed the king of all that happened. He was terribly distressed, and at once he summoned a man named Araches, who was next in authority to the king, and his chief counsellor. He bade him not to be grieved at the occurrence, for that Joasaph would speedily renounce the faith. He counselled him in the first instance to send out soldiers to seize Barlaam, so that he might be put to a terrible death. The king adopted this advice, and the soldiers sought far and near

for Barlaam ; Araches himself went off with a large
band of horsemen to the land of Shinar in search of him.
They traversed mountains and valleys and places difficult of access in their vain efforts. At length, having
ascended a height, Araches discerned a company of
hermits walking along. He at once sent his men to lay
hold on them. " *They came around them like dogs,*" and
like wild beasts eager for the slaughter ; but when they
brought them to Araches he perceived that Barlaam was
not amongst them, for he knew his appearance. He
enquired of them if they knew him and where he was.
They told him they knew him well, as he was their
brother and comrade, but what had become of him they
could not tell. Araches refused to believe them, and he
cruelly tortured them in the endeavour to force them to
speak. When he had failed in his attempt, he brought
them before the king, who threatened them with death if
they did not inform him where Barlaam was to be found.
They fearlessly witnessed for the faith, and having
refused to obey the king or to be influenced by his
threats, he had them cruelly martyred.

Now since the first plan which they devised had failed,
the king said to Araches that some other expedient must
be tried, and he bade him summon a counsellor named
Nachor to see what advice he would give. Araches went
in search of him at dead of night ; and having found
him in a cave where he practised divination, they
arranged their plans together, and in the morning he
returned to the king. Starting off once more under the
pretence of looking for Barlaam, Araches saw an old
man coming out of a ravine. He sent his attendants to
seize him, and when he was brought near to him, he
asked him who he was and what was his religion. He
answered that he was a Christian and that his name was

Barlaam (for this was the plot that had been devised). Thereupon he carried him off to the king, who told him that he might justly put him to death at once, but that in mercy he would allow him some time to make up his mind whether he would obey his orders or else die in cruel pain.

Meantime the news spread abroad that Barlaam had been arrested, and when the prince heard of it he was terribly distressed, and with bitter tears he besought God to aid the aged man in his time of need. His prayer was heard, and a vision was vouchsafed to him which revealed the plot, so that when he awoke, his sorrow was turned into joy.

Two days after this the king came to see his son; he refrained from his usual greeting, and with an angry and sorrowful countenance he asked him whether he had brought shame and trouble upon him by embracing the religion which he hated and persecuted. The prince answered that he would make no secret of what he had done; that he had been brought out of darkness into light; and that, forsaking the worship of idols, he had been enrolled amongst the disciples of Christ. As the king heard his words he was very angry; "Truly," he cried, "did the astrologers at your birth foretell that you would turn out an utterly wicked man—self-willed and disobedient to your parents; and now if you defeat my counsel and show yourself unmindful of your duty to me, I shall turn against you, and treat you as no one would treat even his worst enemy." The prince calmly but firmly answered that come what might he could not deny his Lord; and then the king threatened him once more and went away. He consulted now again with Araches, and told him how steadfast the prince was in his determination not to renounce the faith; and they agreed together that the king should try the effect of adopting a different kind of treatment. Accordingly the day after, he summoned his son to his presence ; he greeted him most affectionately, and besought of him to remember the duty of obeying his father ; he told him how carefully he had himself sought out the path of truth, and that after investigating the matter he had become convinced that the religion of the Galilæans and their attitude towards this present world were alike false ; so he entreated him to comply with his wishes and to be guided by his advice. The prince admitted the duty of obedience to parents, but he told his father that there was a duty still higher, and that in a matter of right and wrong he must obey God rather than man.

And now the king perceived that neither by threats nor by persuasions could he induce his son to forsake the faith, and so he said to him, " You ought to obey my commands, and yield to my wishes ; but since you refuse, let us hold a public assembly. Barlaam who imposed upon you is my prisoner ; I shall promulgate a decree for all the Christians to gather together here, and I shall promise them security from harm. We shall then discuss the whole matter ; and either you and your Barlaam shall persuade us, or else we shall win you over to obedience to my orders." Guided by the heavenly vision, the prince consented to this plan ; and so the proclamations were issued ; but of the Christians, there was but one, named Barachias, who came to help the supposed Barlaam. Some of them were too old ; others were hidden away in distant mountains and caves ; and others again were too much afraid of the king to venture to come.

A vast throng of idolaters gathered together and consulted one with another against the prince and those

who thought with him ; and the proverb was fulfilled
which speaks of a roe fighting with a lion.   For he made
the Most High his refuge, and trusted in the shadow of
His wings ; they trusted in the rulers of this world, and
the prince of darkness, who had most grievously enslaved
them.

Nachor was now brought out, who was pretending that
he was Barlaam.   And then the king proclaimed to his
orators and philosophers, "Here is a controversy set
before you upon which most momentous issues depend,
for either of two things shall happen.   If you win
victory for our religion, and convict Barlaam and his
associates of error, you shall be greatly honoured by us
and by the whole assembly ; and you shall be adorned
with crowns of victory.   But if you are worsted, you
shall be in shame put to a terrible death ; your property
shall be confiscated ; the memorial of you shall be taken
from the earth ; your bodies shall be cast to wild beasts,
and your children shall be condemned to perpetual
slavery."

When the king had thus spoken, the prince arose and
said, "O king, you have judged justly, and may the
Lord confirm your purpose.   Now I shall speak to my
teacher."   Turning then to Nachor, who was feigning
himself to be Barlaam, he said to him, "You know in
what royal dignity you found me, and how under the
influence of your teaching, I forsook the customs and
traditions of my country, and brought upon myself my
father's anger.   Now remember you have to make your
choice : if you vanquish in the argument, and convince
our opponents they are wrong, I shall think more of you
than ever ; I shall regard you as a herald of the truth ;
and I shall remain true to the Christian faith until I die.
But if through craft, or in reality, you are defeated, I

M

shall speedily take vengeance upon you. With my own hands, I shall tear out your heart and tongue, and cast your body to the dogs, so that others may be warned not to deceive a king's son."

When Nachor heard this, he was stricken with fear, and as he thought over the matter, he determined to defend the cause of the prince, lest he should really carry out his threats. But the whole course of events was guided by the providence of God ; for when the king's orators assembled for the discussion, then Nachor arose, and, beckoning with his hand to the multitude to keep silence, he opened his mouth, and, like Balaam's ass, he spoke words such as his own heart never suggested. For he said that the inhabitants of the world might be divided into three classes — Polytheists, Jews, and Christians ; and that of Polytheists, there were three divisions — Chaldæans, Greeks, and Egyptians. The Chaldæans worshipped different objects in nature, which they represented in works of art, and placed in their temples. The elements of nature, however, cannot be gods, for they are liable to corruption and change. The sky cannot be a god, for it moves; it is subject to law, and it is composite; for this reason it is called kosmos. Now kosmos is that which is formed by an artificer ; and what is formed has of necessity a beginning and an end. The motion of the heavenly bodies and the alternation of seasons prove that the sky is subject to law. It is not a god, but the work of God.

The earth cannot be god, for it can be injured by men, by fire, and by rain ; it can be trodden under foot by man, and polluted in many ways.

Water cannot be a god, for it is subservient to human use, and assumes different forms and colours. Fire cannot be a god, for it also is subject to man ; it can be carried about, employed for one purpose or another, and be put out. Wind cannot be a god, for it is given by God to carry the ships over the sea, and by His bidding it rises and falls. The sun cannot be a god, for it moves across the sky, it rises and sets, it has its orbit as well as the other heavenly bodies, it is liable to be eclipsed, and it has no control over its own motion. Nor can the moon be a god, for it is inferior to the sun, and subject to still greater changes. Man cannot be a god, for laws are imposed upon him ; he is the victim of evil passions, of disease, of old age, and death. The religion of the Chaldæans must therefore be false.

The Greeks, who claim to be very wise, are more foolish even than the Chaldæans ; they believe in a multitude of deities—some of them male, others female—and they regard them as the victims of all kinds of passion, and the perpetrators of every crime.

The Egyptians are still worse ; for, not content with such objects of adoration as are worshipped by the Chaldæans and Greeks, they regard irrational animals, both beasts and fishes, as gods, and trees and plants as well.

The Jews received, indeed, the knowledge of the true God, but they proved themselves ungrateful and rebellious ; and they crucified the Son of God, notwithstanding His mighty works done on their behalf.

But the Christians regard themselves as sprung from Christ Himself; in Him they believe, and their belief gives them their name ; they follow His teaching, and this is indeed the way of truth, which leads those who follow it to life eternal.

The king was terribly incensed by Nachor's words ; yet he was powerless, for by his own proclamation he had given liberty to the Christians to speak freely. He tried by signs to convey to him that he must take the other side, but he only became still more eloquent : and finally, as it was now evening, the discussion was adjourned until the following day. As the assembly broke up, the prince requested that his teacher might be allowed to remain with him that night, and when the king consented, he brought him to his palace. Then he told him that he knew well that he was not Barlaam, but Nachor the astrologer. He reminded him of what he had involuntarily uttered that day, and he spent the night urging him to forsake his astrology and idolatry and to embrace the faith of Christ. Nachor at length yielded. He promised that he would see the king's face no more, and early in the morning he left the palace, and journeyed until he found the secret abode of one of the hermits, by whom he was baptized.

Next day the king heard of his departure, and consequently he knew that his plan had utterly failed. He cruelly tortured the philosophers who had been defeated in the argument ; and now he began to recognize how weak those gods must be whom he had worshipped, though as yet he would not open his eyes to receive light from Christ. For some time after these events the prince was allowed to live at peace in his palace. But then it came to pass that a great festival in honour of the idols was about to be held in the city. The priests perceived that the king had grown cold in his attachment to his religion, and they feared that he would not come to the feast, and that they would lose his customary gifts. They went off, therefore, to a very clever man, named Theudas, who was a zealous idolater, and they asked him to interfere on their behalf. Theudas presented himself before the king, and when he had told him how all his plans to win back his son had failed, Theudas counselled him to remove

the present attendants of the prince, and to substitute
very beautiful women in their stead to allure him through
the lusts of the flesh. "For," he said, "there was once a
king who was in great trouble because he had no son.
And when in course of time a boy was born to him, his
heart was filled with joy. The physicians, however, told
him that the appearance of the child's eyes was such that
if for twelve years he saw the sun or fire he would lose
his sight. And so for twelve years the king kept him
shut up in the dark recesses of a cave into which no ray
of light could penetrate. When the twelve years were
over he was brought out, and the king determined to make
a great display, and to show him in succession all those
things which he had never seen as yet. Each object was
to be set in a place by itself—men, women, silver, gold,
pearls, precious stones, beautiful dresses, a chariot har-
nessed with the king's horses, herds of oxen, and flocks
of sheep. The boy asked what each thing was, and when
he inquired the name given to women, the king's armour-
bearer answered in jest that they were called demons,
because they led men astray. But the boy was more
impressed by them than by anything else ; and so, when
they brought him back to the king, and the king asked
him what he liked best, the boy answered, 'Why, those
demons who lead men astray, for nothing that I saw to-
day delighted my heart as much as they did.' And the
king was astonished, and he perceived what a tyranny
the love of woman exercises over the heart of man. Now
it will be by this means that you will overcome your son's
resolution."

The king adopted this advice, and comely, beautiful
maidens were brought before him. He gave orders that
they should be arrayed in gorgeous attire, and removing
all the attendants of the prince, he substituted them in

their place, so that he had no one else with whom he could converse or take his meals. Theudas went off to his cave, and by his incantations he summoned an evil spirit, who took with him other spirits more wicked than himself, and went to the chamber of the prince to kindle the flame of fleshly desire, while the women, by their allurements, supplied the fuel.

The noble youth, in earnest prayer, sought deliverance from the snare that was laid for him, so that he might not stain the fair garment wherewith his baptism had encircled him. And thus by supplication and by fasting and self-mortification, he overcame the temptation, and disappointed the expectation of the enemy of his soul. Then a still stronger temptation was presented before him, for there was one maiden, most beautiful and in-telligent—a king's daughter—carried captive from her own country, and brought as a gift to King Abener. She was now sent to the prince, in order that she might succeed where the other women had failed. When he saw her approaching, he at once appealed to her to serve the living God, and to be wedded to the immortal Bridegroom. As she heard his words, she asked him if he was so desirous for her salvation, to grant her request and take her to be his wife. And when he indignantly refused, she said to him, "Why do you say this when you are so wise? How can you describe marriage as a defilement and an impurity? I am not unacquainted with Christian books; I read many of them in my own country, and I heard Christians speak. Is it not then written in some of your Books, '*Marriage is honourable, and the bed undefiled;*' and again, '*It is better to marry than to burn;*' and again, '*What God hath joined together let no man put asunder*'? Do not your Scrip-tures say that all the saints of olden time, patriarchs and prophets, were married? Is it not written that Peter, the chief of the Apostolic band, had a wife? How can you then call it a defilement? You seem to contradict your own Scriptures." He replied that marriage was lawful for all save for those who had taken a vow of celibacy, and that when he was baptized and had been cleansed from the sins of his youthful ignorance, he had made this promise. She then tempted him for once to yield to her desires, holding out to him the prospect that by so doing he would bring about her salvation, since she in return would embrace the Christian faith. He felt his resolution failing him, and as the enemy summoned all his power to compass his ruin, he again sought refuge in prayer. As he prayed he fell asleep, and in a vision he was permitted to behold first the fields of glory and the city adorned with gold and precious stones, and then the dread abode of those who shall be cast into darkness. He awoke, trembling violently, and immediately the beauty of the shameless maiden and of all the rest appeared to him more disgusting than what was defiled and decayed ; and calling to mind the vision, in his desire for heaven and his fear of hell, he lay upon his bed unable to move.*

* It is interesting to notice how closely the narrative here follows on Buddhist lines. Not only is there the temptation to which the Buddha was exposed, according to the Legends, from the three daughters of Maro, as a foundation for this incident, but still more exactly in "The Legend of Lomasa Kasyápa" (Spence Hardy's Manual of Buddhism, page 51), it is related that Sakra, through jealousy, wished to set aside the merit of this rishi ; and that he induced the king to endeavour to persuade him to offer a sacrifice. When he refused, Sakra again appeared to the king, and recommended him to send his daughter Chandrawati-Déwi to make the same request. The princess was most beautifully arrayed, and sent to the forest. At the sight of the princess, the rishi forgot his obligations, and consented to accompany her to the city. On their

Now when the king heard that he was lying sick, he came to visit him; but the prince, as he beheld his father, reproached him for the snares that he had laid for him, and he besought the king to allow him to leave the palace, and to go forth into the desert that he might find Barlaam, his friend and teacher. The king was exceedingly grieved, it seemed as if all his efforts had failed; but he determined not to give up until he had made another attempt. Accordingly he summoned Theudas once more to his presence, and enquired of him if he could suggest any further expedient. Theudas requested that he might be allowed himself to have an interview with the prince. The king gave his consent, and in the morning they both came to visit him. Theudas vehemently reproached him for abandoning the worship of idols. But the prince replied to his statements by exposing the senseless folly of idolatry, and in contrast with such superstition he set the pure faith of the gospel of Christ. Theudas, while he listened, was smitten, as it were, by a thunderbolt; he remained silent for awhile, then turning to the king he cried, "Truly, O king, the Spirit of God dwells in thy son; we are overcome and left powerless to defend our position; we cannot shut our eyes to the force of his statements. Great is the God of the Christians; great their faith; great their mysteries." He then asked the prince whether God would receive him in spite of all his evil deeds; and

---

arrival, the animals were all assembled in the place of sacrifice; but when he lifted up the knife to slay the elephant, the affrighted beast cried out, and all the rest joined in the lamentation. This brought the rishi to his senses, and, throwing down the knife, he fled at once to the forest, where he accomplished the requisite amount of merit, and was afterwards born in a brahma-lóka. This rishi was the Bodhisat who afterwards became Gotama Buddha.

when he had assured him that he would receive the welcome promised to every repentant sinner, he went out of the palace to his cave, where he burned all that appertained to his magical arts. He then sought out Nachor, from whom he received further instruction, and after some time he was baptized.

Now these events made the king still more perplexed, and he summoned his Council so as to know what they should advise. Then Araches, who has been already mentioned, counselled him to divide his kingdom with the prince. He pointed out that the cares of government might distract the youth from his religious zeal, but that even if this did not happen the king would have the satisfaction of feeling that his son had not been altogether lost to him. The king eagerly adopted the plan, and to his great joy the prince consented to the proposal. He told his father that he had intended to renounce everything, and to seek some friend with whom to spend the remainder of his days, but that this was a matter in which it was both right and wise for him to comply with his father's wishes.

And so the kingdom was divided, and the father made his son king, and gave him a royal retinue. He apportioned to him a large and populous city for his abode, and he left nothing wanting to enhance his dignity and pomp.

Joasaph went to his city, and he placed the sign of our Lord's Passion, that is the sacred Cross of Christ, on every tower it contained ; he overthrew the temples and altars of the idols ; he built a large and beautiful church, dedicated to Christ the Lord, in the midst of the city, and enjoined the people frequently to come there, and to offer worship to God through adoration of the Cross. He was himself foremost in acts of public worship ; he did everything to turn people from idolatry and to lead them

to Christ. He preached the Gospel; the infinite con-
descension of God the Word; the wonder of His Incarnation; His suffering the cross, whereby we are saved;
His ascension to heaven and His return to judge the
quick and the dead.

So gentle was his character and so just his government
that multitudes were led by his influence to renounce
idolatry. Priests and monks and a few bishops, hearing
of him, came forth from their hiding places and resorted
to his city. One of these bishops, who had been driven
away by persecution from his own see, he appointed
to the Church recently constructed. He made a
baptistery, and in it a great multitude were baptized,
both rulers and civil officers, soldiers and people;* and
those who were baptized received not only spiritual
blessing, but deliverance from every bodily disease that
had come upon them. Thus his kingdom increased, and
Joasaph devoted himself entirely to the welfare of his
people. He ministered to the poor; he visited the
prisoners, both those who were condemned to the mines,
and those who were in bondage for debt; he was the
friend of the widow and the orphan, and the helper of all
who were in distress. His fame spread more and more,
until at length those who were subject to his father's rule
attached themselves to him, so that the house of Joasaph
grew stronger and stronger, and the house of Abener
grew weaker and weaker, just as the Book of the Kings
relates concerning David and Saul. When Abener
perceived this he was more than ever convinced of the
powerlessness of the idols. Once more he summoned
his Council; and now he informed them that he had

---

* Note the apparent allusion here to the Caste divisions of the
Indian people.

made up his mind to embrace Christianity. They all assented to his views and he forthwith sent a letter to Joasaph to tell him what he was about to do.

He received the letter with intense joy, and having offered his thanksgiving to God, he set out to visit his father. When he heard that his son was coming, he went forth to meet him ; he welcomed him most warmly, and celebrated his arrival by a public festival. A long conference then took place in private between the father and the son, with the result that Joasaph summoned the Bishop, of whom mention has been made, to baptize the king. Joasaph acted as his sponsor, and thus the strange result was brought to pass that he became father to his own father, for he led to spiritual regeneration him from whom he had himself derived natural life.

And now the king was zealous to use all his efforts to promote the well-being of the Christians. He bitterly lamented his former acts of cruelty towards them, and it needed all Joasaph's arguments to convince him that he had not sinned too deeply to receive God's forgiveness. Shortly afterwards he died, commending his soul in penitence to the hands of God. Joasaph with tears laid him in a tomb owned by pious men, and he shrouded him, not with his royal robes, but with the garb of penitence. For seven days he offered up prayers at the tomb, beseeching God not to remember his father's former sins, but to extend His infinite mercy to him. Then on the eighth day he returned to his palace, and collecting all his treasures, he distributed them to the poor. He summoned a great assembly of nobles, soldiers, and people, and he told them that formerly he had intended to embrace the ascetic life, but that, in compliance with the earnest desire of his father, he had postponed carrying his purpose into effect. But now that he had died

no difficulty remained, and therefore he intended to
leave them and perform his vow.

Thereupon all the assembly broke into loud utterances
of grief, beseeching him to remain ; nay, further, they
bound themselves by an oath that they would not allow
him to depart. The king with great trouble quieted them
in some measure, and sent them to their homes. He then
summoned Barachias, who stood by Nachor when he was
feigning himself to be Barlaam, and entreated him to
take the kingly office. Barachias absolutely refused,
saying that if it was a good thing he ought to retain it
himself, but that if it was a hindrance he had no right
to thrust it upon him. The king saw that it was useless
to press the matter further, and said nothing more. He
spent the night writing a letter to the people, full of wise
counsel as to the life he would have them live, and
stating that no one but Barachias should succeed to the
throne. He left the letter in his bedchamber, and in the
morning he went forth unknown to all. But when it was
day the news spread, and the whole city went forth to
search everywhere for him. At length they found him in
the bed of a torrent, lifting up his hands to heaven and
saying the prayer appointed for the sixth hour. Once
more they entreated him to return, but he told them it
was useless to urge him, as his resolution could not be
shaken.

He then took Barachias by the hand, and turning
towards the East, he prayed for him, and presented him
to the people as their king. He charged him to govern
in accordance with God's laws ; and now he bade them
all farewell ; and amidst their bitter tears he went forth
upon his way, while they watched him and followed him
at a distance till night hid him from their view.

Thus he left his palace, joyful in heart, like one who

having been long in exile, at length returns to his native
land.   He had on his ordinary dress, but underneath was
the rough garment of hair which Barlaam had given him.
That night he stopped in a poor man's cottage, and to
him he gave the robes he wore, as his final act of charity.
So he went forth to the solitary life, carrying neither
bread, nor water, nor any other of the necessaries of life,
but having his soul transfixed with love to Christ the
Eternal King.   With steadfast purpose he went forward
never looking behind him, till he reached the remote
parts of the desert, and joyful in heart because he had
got rid of the distracting cares of things temporal, which
he had felt to be a burden and a yoke grievous to be
borne.   He prayed that he might be directed to where
Barlaam dwelt.   Thus he journeyed, subsisting on the
scanty fare of the herbs that grew in the desert, but
suffering much from want of water.

And when the devil, who hates and envies the good, saw
how steadfast his purpose was, he tormented him with
manifold temptations.   He brought up before him in
memory his former glory, his friends and comrades, and
all the pleasures of life ; then he suggested to him
how rough was the path of virtue, how many its difficulties ; he reminded him how weak he was, how
intense was his thirst, how hopeless to expect any
comfort or cessation of toil.   Thus he filled his heart
with thoughts like a cloud of dust, just as it is recorded
concerning the famous Antony.   When this plan failed,
he endeavoured to terrify him.   He appeared before
him black as he really is ; then he rushed towards
him, holding a drawn sword in his hand, and threaten-
ing to strike him if he did not turn back ; then he
assumed the form of different wild beasts, bellowing
and roaring with awe-inspiring sound ; then he changed

himself into a dragon, a serpent, a basilisk. But he remained unmoved through all the ordeal, as one who had made the Most High his refuge. He rebuked the evil one, and making the sign of the Cross, the beasts and reptiles vanished like smoke, or like wax before the fire. And once more he went on his way, and though he encountered many dangers, his heart was unmoved, for with him love had cast out fear.

He at length reached the land of Shinar, where Barlaam lived. For two years he there sought for him in vain, wandering up and down in the vast wilderness; then most earnestly he prayed again to be directed to his abode. Through Divine Providence he came across a monk who lived alone in a cave, and from him he learned where Barlaam was to be found. Standing outside the cave where he was told that he dwelt, he cried, "Bless me, father, bless me!" Barlaam came forth, and in spirit recognized him whose external appearance was so changed by the hardships he had undergone that he could scarcely be thought to be the same person. Joasaph recognized him also. Then the aged man gave thanks to God, turning towards the East, and at the end of the prayer they said "Amen," and they embraced one another in deep joy at meeting again after their long separation.

In answer to Barlaam's inquiry, Joasaph told him all that had happened since he left him ; then once more he gave thanks that the seed had fallen into such good ground and brought forth such abundant fruit.

Joasaph lived for a considerable time with Barlaam, practising asceticism to such an extent that even Barlaam was smitten with wonder, and felt himself inferior to him in his severe self-discipline. He never lost an hour, nay even not a moment, all the time that

he dwelt in the desert.   For this is the duty of the
monastic order, never to suffer themselves to intermit
spiritual exercise.

After a long time had passed, one day Barlaam told
Joasaph that he felt that the hour of his death was at
hand.   He asked him to lay his body in the earth, and
to pray for him, lest his many sins of ignorance might
retard the progress of his soul , and he exhorted Joasaph
to persevere to the end in the course of life which he
had adopted.   He procured what was necessary for the
holy sacrifice, and presented to God the bloodless
Offering, and, having communicated himself, he administered to Joasaph the pure Mysteries of Christ.
Then he spent the night comforting him in his sorrow
at his approaching death ; and in the morning he offered
prayer to God, and having made the sign of the Cross,
he died peacefully, as though he were setting out upon a
happy journey.

Joasaph, in deepest sorrow, committed his body with
all reverence to the ground ; he recited over him the
customary Psalms ; and, in his loneliness, he betook
himself to prayer.   He then fell asleep, and it seemed
to him as though he was borne again to that glorious
city which he had seen before.   When he entered into it,
beings wreathed with light met him, holding in their hands
crowns of wondrous beauty, such as mortal eyes have
never seen.   As he asked for whom they were intended,
the answer came that one was for himself, since he had
led so many souls to salvation, and since he now was
devoting himself so fully to the ascetic life ; and that a
second crown was his also, which he might give to his
father whom he had turned from his evil ways.   Joasaph
indignantly exclaimed, "How can you make him equal
to me, when I have endured so much, and he performed

but one act of penitence?" But Barlaam appeared to
him, and reproved him, "Did I not tell you that when
you were very rich, you would not be liberal, and you
were astonished at my words; yet now, instead of re-
joicing, you are indignant that your father is set on an
equality with you?" Then Joasaph sought pardon, and
he asked Barlaam where he dwelt, and he told him he
dwelt in that most beautiful city, and the abode which
was allotted to him was in a street in the midst of it,
radiant with most brilliant light, and that Joasaph would
come there also if he persevered to the end, as soon as
he was set free from the burden of the flesh. Then he
awoke, comforted and strengthened by the vision.

To the end he maintained the ascetic life; he was
twenty-five years old when he left his palace, and for
thirty and five years he lived as a hermit. When his
course was finished, he died in peace, and obtained
the crown of glory. The monk who had told him
where Barlaam abode, was informed by Divine revelation of what was taking place; he came in just as
Joasaph had died, then he fulfilled the Christian rites,
and laid him in the grave with Barlaam, his father.
In obedience to a vision, the monk journeyed to
India, and informed Barachias of what had happened.
Then a great multitude set out without delay to visit
the tomb, and having found the bodies of Barlaam
and Joasaph free from all corruption, and entirely un-
changed, the king ordered them to be placed in splendid coffins, and to be carried back to his country.
When this reached the ears of the people, a vast throng
out of every city and district assembled to view and
to worship the blessed bodies. They sang hymns of
praise over them, and lighted many torches (suitably,
as one might say, putting lights around the sons and

heirs of light), and laid them in the Church built by Joasaph. And the Lord wrought many wonders and cures by their bones, both while the bodies were being removed and buried, and also in after days. And King Barachias and all the people saw these wonders ; and many of the surrounding nations who were unbelievers, and did not know the Lord, were convinced by the miracles at the tomb. And all who saw and heard, marvelled at the angelic life of Joasaph and his all-pervading love to God ; and they glorified God who ever works with those who love Him, and rewards them with priceless gifts.

Now this is the end of the book, which I have written to the best of my ability, as I heard it from the worthy men who truthfully related it to me. May we who read or hear this profitable story, receive our portion together with those holy men, Barlaam and Joasaph, who, by prayer and intercession, pleased God through Jesus Christ our Lord, to whom be honour, power, majesty, and glory, with the Father and the Holy Spirit, now and ever, and throughout all ages. Amen.

N

APPENDIX II.

Did Buddhism Influence Early Christianity?

THE question of the influence of Buddhism upon primitive Christianity can be best decided by considering (1) the parallel passages between the Holy Scriptures and the Buddhist Sacred Books. In the list I have quoted both from the Pâli Pi*t*akas, and from the later Buddhist Books, some of which date subsequently to the Christian era; (2) the points of contact and of contrast between Christian and Buddhist teaching; (3) the supposed influence of Buddhism upon early Christianity; (4) Buddhism and the Canonical Gospels; and (5) the similarity between Christian and Buddhist asceticism.

1. *List of Parallel Passages between the Holy Scriptures and the Buddhist Sacred Books :—*

Dhammapada.

5. For hatred does not cease by hatred; hatred ceases by love; this is an old rule.

223. Let a man overcome anger by love, let him overcome evil with good; let him overcome the greedy by liberality, the liar by truth.

Rom. xii. 20, 21, "Therefore if thine enemy hunger, feed him; if he thirst, give him to drink, for in so doing thou shalt heap coals of fire upon his head. Be not overcome of evil, but overcome evil with good."

13. As rain breaks through an ill-thatched house, passion will break through an unreflecting mind.

Prov. xxv. 28, "He that hath no rule over his own spirit is like a city that is broken down and without walls."

18. The virtuous man is happy in this world and he is happy in the next ; he is happy in both.

1 Tim. iv. 8, "Godliness is profitable for all things, having promise of the life which now is, and of that which is to come."

19. The thoughtless man, even if he can recite a large portion (of the law), but is not a doer of it, has no share in the priesthood, but is like a cowherd counting the cows of others.

St. James i. 22-24, "Be ye doers of the word, and not hearers only, deceiving your own selves. For if any be a hearer of the word and not a doer, he is like a man beholding his natural face in a glass. For he beholdeth himself and goeth his way and straightway forgetteth what manner of man he was."

40. Knowing that the body is (fragile) like a jar, and making this thought firm as a fortress, one should attack Mâra (the tempter) with the weapon of knowledge, one should watch him when conquered, and should never rest.

St. Matt. xxvi. 41, "Watch and pray, that ye enter not into temptation : the spirit indeed is willing, but the flesh is weak."

50. Not the perversities of others, not their sins of commission or omission, but

St. Matt. vii. 3, "Why beholdest thou the mote that is in thy brother's eye,

his own misdeeds and negligences should a sage take notice of.

62. "These sons belong to me, and this wealth belongs to me," with such thoughts a fool is tormented. He himself does not belong to himself, how much less sons and wealth?

69. As long as the evil deed done does not bear fruit the fool thinks it is like honey; but when it ripens, then the fool suffers grief.

85. Few are there who arrive at the other shore (become Arhats); the other people here run up and down the shore.

103. If one man conquer in battle a thousand times thousand men, and if another conquer himself, he is the greatest of conquerors.

116. If a man would hasten towards the good, he should keep his thought away from evil; if a man does what is good slothfully, his mind delights in evil.

121. Let no man think lightly of evil, saying in his heart, It will not come nigh

and considerest not the beam that is in thine own eye?"

St. Luke xii. 19, 20, "Soul, thou hast much goods laid up for many years. . . . Thou fool, this night thy soul shall be required of thee."

Prov. xx. 17, "Bread of deceit is sweet to a man; but afterwards his mouth shall be filled with gravel."

St. Matt. vii. 14, "Narrow is the gate and straitened the way that leadeth unto life, and few be they that find it."

Prov. xvi. 32, "He that is slow to anger is greater than the mighty, and he that ruleth his spirit than he that taketh a city."

Prov. iv. 23, "Keep thy heart with all diligence, for out of it are the issues of life"; xxiv. 9, "The thought of foolishness is sin."

Eccles. viii. 11, "Because sentence against an evil work is not executed speedily,

me. Even by the falling of waterdrops a waterpot is filled ; the fool becomes full of evil, even if he gather it little by little.

124. He who has no wound on his hand, may touch poison with his hand ; poison does not affect one who has no wound ; nor is there evil for one who does not commit evil.

127. Not in the sky, not in the midst of the sea, not if we enter into the clefts of the mountains is there known a spot in the whole world where a man might be freed from an evil deed.

133. Do not speak harshly to anybody ; those who are spoken to will answer thee in the same way. Angry speech is painful, blows for blows will touch thee.

158. Let each man direct himself first to what is proper, then let him teach others ; thus a wise man will not suffer.

159. If a man make himself as he teaches others to be, then, being himself well-

therefore the heart of the sons of men is fully set to do evil."

Titus i. 15, " To the pure all things are pure."

Num. xxxii. 23, " Be sure your sin will find you out."

Eccles. xii. 14, " God shall bring every work into judgment with every secret thing, whether it be good or whether it be evil."

Prov. xv. 1, " A soft answer turneth away wrath, but grievous words stir up anger.

1 Tim. iv. 16, " Take heed to thyself and to thy teaching. Continue in these things ; for in doing this thou shalt save both thyself and them that hear thee."

St. Luke vi. 39, 40, " Can the blind lead the blind, shall they not both fall into

subdued, he may subdue (others); one's own self is indeed difficult to subdue.

163. Bad deeds and deeds hurtful to ourselves are easy to do; what is beneficial and good, that is very difficult to do.

165. By oneself the evil is done, by oneself one suffers; by oneself evil is left undone, by oneself one is purified. Purity and impurity belong to oneself, no one can purify another.

288. Sons are no help, nor a father, nor relations; there is no help from kinsfolk for one whom death hath seized.

197. Let us live happily, then, not hating those who hate us; among men who hate us let us dwell free from hatred.

207. He who walks in the company of fools suffers a long way; company with fools, as with an enemy, is

the ditch? The disciple is not above his master, but every one when he is perfected shall be as his master."

St. Matt. vii. 13, "Enter ye in by the narrow gate: for wide is the gate and broad is the way that leadeth to destruction . . . narrow is the gate and straitened the way that leadeth unto life."

Ezek. xviii. 20, "The soul that sinneth it shall die . . . the righteousness of the righteous shall be upon him."

Psa. xlix. 7, "None of them can by any means redeem his brother, nor give to God a ransom for him."

Gal. vi. 5, "Each man shall bear his own burden."

St. Luke vi. 27, "Love your enemies; do good to them that hate you."

Prov. xiii. 20, "Walk with wise men and thou shalt be wise; but the companion of fools shall smart for it."

always painful ; company with the wise is pleasure, like meeting with kinsfolk.

252. The fault of others is easily perceived, but that of oneself is difficult to perceive ; a man winnows his neighbour's faults like chaff, but his own fault he hides, as a cheat hides the bad die from the gambler.

St. Matt. vii. 3, "Why beholdest thou the mote that is in thy brother's eye, and considerest not the beam that is in thine own eye ? "

277-279. "All created things perish ; all created things are grief and pain ; all forms are unreal."

Eccles. i. 14, " I have seen all the works that are done under the sun, and behold all is vanity and a striving after wind."

292. What ought to be done is neglected, what ought not to be done is done.

Rom. vii. 19, " The good that I would, I do not, but the evil that I would not, that I do."

297. The disciples of Gotama are always well awake, and their thoughts day and night are always set on the law.

Psa. i. 2, " But his delight is in the law of the Lord, and in His law doth he meditate day and night."

306. He who says what is not, goes to hell ; he also, who having done a thing, says, I have not done it. After death both are equal, they are men with evil deeds in the next world.

Rev. xxi. 8, "All liars shall have their part in the lake that burneth with brimstone and fire, which is the second death."

307. Many men whose shoulders are covered with

St. Matt. vii. 15, " Beware of false prophets which

the yellow gown are ill-con-
ditioned and unrestrained ;
such evil-doers by their
evil deeds go to hell.

313. If anything is to be
done, let a man do it, let
him attack it vigorously.

320. Silently shall I en-
dure abuse, as the elephant
in battle endures the arrow
sent from the bow ; for the
world is ill-natured.

338. As a tree, even
though it has been cut down,
is firm so long as its root is
safe, and grows again.

354. The gift of the law
exceeds all gifts ; the sweetness of the law exceeds all
sweetness ; the delight in
the law exceeds all delights.

389. No one should attack
a Brâhma*n*a, but no Brâhma*n*a (if attacked) should
let himself fly at his ag-
gressor.

394. What is the use of
plaited hair, O fool, what of
the raiment of goat-skins ?
Within thee there is ravening, but the outside thou
makest clean.

come to you in sheep's
clothing, but inwardly they
are ravening wolves."

Eccles. ix. 10, "Whatso-
ever thy hand findeth to do,
do it with thy might."

Psa. xxxix. 1, 2, "I said,
I will take heed to my ways
that I sin not with my
tongue.   I will keep my
mouth as it were with a
bridle, while the wicked is
before me."

Job xiv. 7, "For there is
hope of a tree, if it be cut
down, that it will sprout
again."

Psa. xix. 10, "More to be
desired are they than gold,
yea, than much fine gold :
sweeter also than honey and
the honeycomb."

St. Matt. v. 39, "But I
say unto you, Resist not him
that is evil ; but whosoever
smiteth thee on one cheek,
turn to him the other also."

St. Luke xi. 39, 40, "Now
do ye Pharisees make clean
the outside of the cup and
the platter : but your inward
part is full of ravening and
wickedness.   Ye fools, did

396. I do not call a man a Brâhma*n*a because of his origin or of his mother.

399. Him I call indeed a Brâhma*n*a who, though he has committed no offence, endures reproach, bonds and stripes.

SUTTA NIPÂTA.
Mettasutta.

149. Let him [*i.e.*, the aspirant for Nirvâ*n*a] cultivate goodwill towards all the world, a boundless (friendly) mind, above, and below, and across, unobstructed without hatred, without enmity.

Âmagandhasutta.

241-244. Destroying living beings, killing, cutting, binding, stealing, speaking falsehood, fraud and deception, worthless reading, intercourse with another's wife; this is Âmagandha [*i.e.*, that which defiles], but not the eating of flesh. Anger, intoxication, obstinacy, bigotry, deceit, envy, grandiloquence, pride, conceit, intimacy with the un-

not he that made that which is without make that which is within also?"

Rom. ii. 28, "He is not a Jew which is one outwardly."

1 St. Pet. ii. 20, "If when ye do well, and suffer for it, ye take it patiently, this is acceptable with God."

St. Luke vi. 27, "Love your enemies, do good to them that hate you, bless them that curse you, pray for them that despitefully use you."

St. Matt. xv. 11, 19, "Not that which entereth into the mouth defileth the man; but that which proceedeth out of the mouth, this defileth the man. For out of the heart come forth evil thoughts, murders, adulteries, fornications, thefts, false witness, railings.

just—this is what defiles.

[The whole section of this Discourse is an expansion of the thought that defilement is moral, not ceremonial.]

248. Neither the flesh of fish, nor fasting, nor nakedness, nor tonsure, nor matted hair, nor dirt, nor rough skins, nor the worshipping of the fire, nor the many immortal penances in the world, nor hymns, nor oblations, nor sacrifice, nor observance of the seasons, purify a mortal who has not conquered his doubt.

1 Sam. xv. 22, "Behold, to obey is better than sacrifice."

Isa. i. 13, "Bring no more vain oblations : incense is an abomination unto Me ; the new moons and Sabbaths, the calling of assemblies, I cannot away with ; it is iniquity, even the solemn meeting."

Gal. iv. 10, "Ye observe days and months and times and years, I am afraid of you lest I have bestowed upon you labour in vain."

Dhammikasutta.

393. Let [the lay disciple] not kill, nor cause to be killed any living being, nor let him approve of others killing, after having refrained from hurting all creatures, both those that are strong and those that tremble in the world.

Exod. xx. 13, "Thou shalt do no murder."

394. Then let him abstain from (taking) anything in any place that has not been

Exod. xx. 15, "Thou shalt not steal."

given (to him), knowing (it to belong to another), let him not cause any one to take, nor approve of those that take, let him avoid all (sort of) theft.

395. Let the wise man avoid an unchaste life, as a burning heap of coals ; not being able to live a life of chastity, let him not transgress with another man's wife.

Exod. xx. 14, "Thou shalt not commit adultery."

Compare Prov. vi. 28, 29, " Can one go upon hot coals and his feet not be burned ? So he that goeth in to his neighbour's wife : whosoever toucheth her shall not be innocent."

396. Let no one speak falsely of another in the hall of justice or in the hall of the assembly, let him not cause (any one) to speak (falsely), nor approve of those that speak (falsely), let him avoid all (sort of) untruth.

Exod. xx. 16, "Thou shalt not bear false witness against thy neighbour."

397. Let the householder who approves of this Dhamma, not give himself to intoxicating drinks ; let him not cause others to drink, nor approve of those that drink, knowing it to end in madness.

Eph. v. 18, "Be not drunk with wine, wherein is excess."

Isa. v. 11, "Woe unto them that rise up early in the morning that they may follow strong drink."

Hab. ii. 15, "Woe unto him that giveth his neighbour drink."

402. Let a wise man with a believing mind, gladdening the assembly of the Bhikkhus with food and drink, make distributions according to his ability.

Heb. xiii. 16, "To do good and to distribute forget not."

403. Let him dutifully maintain his parents, and practise an honourable trade; the householder who observes this strenuously goes to the gods by name Sayampabhas.

Exod. xx. 12, "Honour thy father and thy mother, that thy days may be long upon the land which the Lord thy God giveth thee."

Mâghasutta.

487. He who is a liberal giver, bountiful, suitable to beg of, and who justly seeks for riches, and having sought for riches justly, gives out of his justly obtained and justly acquired riches . . . produces much good.

Prov. xxviii. 27, "He that giveth unto the poor shall not lack."

Dan. iv. 27, "Break off thy sins by righteousness, and thine iniquities by showing mercy to the poor."

574. Without a cause and unknown is the life of mortals in this world, troubled and brief and combined with pain.

Eccles. vi. 12, "Who knoweth what is good for man in this life all the days of his vain life which he spendeth as a shadow? For who can tell a man what shall be after him under the sun?"

575. For there is not any means by which those that have been born can avoid

2 Sam. xiv. 14, "For we must needs die and are as water spilled on the ground,

dying ; after reaching old age there is death, of such a nature are living beings.

577. As all earthen vessels made by the potter end in being broken, so is the life of mortals.

578. Both young and grown-up men, both those who are fools and those who are wise men, all fall into the power of death, all are subject to death. Of those who overcome by death go to the other world, a father does not save his son, nor relatives their relations.

589. Even if a man lives a hundred years, or even more, he is at last separated from the company of his relatives, and leaves life in this world.

666. One's deeds are not lost, they will surely come (back to you), their master will meet with them . . . in the other world.

which cannot be gathered up again."

Heb. ix. 27, "It is appointed unto men once to die."

Eccles. xii. 6, "Or ever the silver cord be loosed, or the golden bowl be broken, or the pitcher be broken at the fountain, or the wheel broken at the cistern."

Psa. xlix. 7, 9, 10, "None of them can by any means redeem his brother, nor give to God a ransom for him, that he should still live alway, that he should not see corruption. For he seeth that wise men die, the fool and the brutish together perish, and leave their wealth to others."

Psa. xc. 10, "The days of our years are threescore years and ten, or even by reason of strength fourscore years ; yet is their pride but labour and sorrow, for it is soon gone and we fly away."

Rev. xiv. 13, "Their works do follow them."

694. My life here will shortly be at an end, in the middle (of his life) then will be death for me; I shall not hear the Dhamma of the incomparable one; therefore I am afflicted, unfortunate, and suffering.

Isa. xxxix. 10, 11, "In the noontide of my days I shall go into the gates of the grave: I am deprived of the residue of my years. I said, I shall not see the Lord, even the Lord in the land of the living."

806. That even of which a man thinks "This is mine," is left behind by death; knowing this, let not the wise (man) turn himself to worldliness (while being my) follower.

Psalm xlix. 17, "When he dieth, he shall carry nothing away; his glory shall not follow after him."

1 Tim. vi. 7, "We brought nothing into this world, and it is certain that we can carry nothing out."

862, 865. Whence (do spring up) contentions and disputes, lamentation and sorrow, together with envy? From wish originate the (dear) objects in the world, and the covetousness that prevails in the world, and desire and fulfilment originate from it.

St. James iv. 1, "From whence come wars and fightings among you? Come they not hence even of your pleasures that war in your members."

937. The world is completely unsubstantial, all quarters are shaken.

1 St. John ii. 17, "The world passeth away, and the lust thereof."

970, 971. "What shall I eat, or where shall I eat?— he lay indeed uncomfortably (last night)—Where shall I

St. Matt. vi. 31, "Be not therefore anxious, saying, What shall we eat? or, what shall we drink? or,

lie this night? Let the Sekha [novice or student] who wanders about houseless, subdue these lamentable doubts. Having had in (due) time both food and clothes, let him know moderation in this world for the sake of happiness.

wherewithal shall we be clothed?"

1 Tim. vi. 8, "Having food and covering, we shall be therewith content."

1073. As a flame blown about by the violence of the wind goes out, even so a Muni [a sage] disappears, and cannot be reckoned as existing.

St. James iv. 14, "What is your life? For ye are a vapour that appeareth for a little while and then vanisheth away."

Mahâvagga.

viii. 26, 3. Whosoever, O Bhikkhus, would wait upon me, he should wait upon the sick.

St. Matt. xxv. 36, 40, " I was sick and ye visited Me. Inasmuch as ye did it unto one of these, My brethren, even these least, ye did it unto Me."

[The parallels which follow are from the Buddhist Books of later date.]

The Saddharma-Puṇḍarîka.

ii. 36. My congregation, Sâriputra, has been cleared from the chaff, freed from the trash ; it is firmly established in the strength of faith.

St. Matt. iii. 12, "Whose fan is in His Hand, and He will throughly purge His floor, and gather His wheat into the garner ; but He will burn up the chaff with unquenchable fire."

ii. 139. Let this mystery

St. Mark xiii. 11, " It is

be for thee, *Sâriputra,* for all disciples of mine, and for the eminent Bodhisattvas, who are to keep this mystery.

iii. 38. I will tell thee a parable, for men of good understanding will generally readily enough catch the meaning of what is taught under the shape of a parable.

iv. We are stricken with wonder, amazement, and rapture at hearing a voice ; it is the lovely voice, the leader's voice, that so unexpectedly we hear to-day. In a short moment we have acquired a heap of precious jewels, such as we were not thinking of nor requiring. All of us are astonished to hear it. It is like (the history of) a young person who, seduced by foolish people, went away from his father, and wandered to another country far distant. The father was sorry to perceive

given unto you to know the mysteries of the kingdom of heaven, but to them it is not given."

St. Matt. xiii. 34, 35, "All these things spake Jesus unto the multitudes in parables, and without a parable spake He not unto them ; that it might be fulfilled which was spoken by the prophet, saying, I will open my mouth in parables ; I will utter things which have been kept secret from the foundation of the world."

St. Luke xv. 11-24, "And He said, A certain man had two sons, and the younger of them said to his father, Father, give me the portion of goods that falleth to me. And he divided unto them

that his son had run away, and in his sorrow roamed the country in all directions during no less than fifty years. In search of his son, he came to some great city, where he built a house and dwelt, blessed with all that can gratify the five senses. . . In such way, the man becomes wealthy ; but he gets old, aged, advanced in years, and he passes days and nights always sorrowful in mind, on account of his son. . . Meanwhile that foolish son is wandering from village to village, poor and miserable, seeking food and clothing. When begging, he at one time gets something, another time he does not. . . In course of time, he, in his rovings, reaches the town where his father is living, and comes to his father's mansion to beg for food and raiment. . . The poor man, seeing the splendid mansion of the householder, thinks within himself, where am I here? This man must be a king or a grandee.

his living. And not many days after, the younger son gathered all together, and took his journey into a far country, and there wasted his substance with riotous living. And when he had spent all, there arose a mighty famine in that land, and he began to be in want. And he went and joined himself to a citizen of that country ; and he sent him into his fields to feed swine. And he would fain have filled his belly with the husks which the swine did eat ; and no man gave unto him. And when he came to himself, he said, How many hired servants of my father's have bread enough, and to spare, and I perish with hunger ! I will arise and go to my father, and will say unto him, Father, I have sinned against heaven, and before thee, and am no more worthy to be called thy son ; make me as one of thy hired servants. And he arose and came to his father. But when he was yet a great

o

Let me not incur some injury, and be caught to do forced labour. With these reflections, he hurried away, inquiring after the road to the street of the poor. The rich man on the throne is glad to see his own son, and despatches messengers with the order to fetch that poor man. The messengers immediately seize the man ; but he is no sooner caught than he faints away (as he thinks): These are certainly executioners who have approached me ; what do I want, clothing or food ? On seeing it, the rich sagacious man (thinks): This ignorant and stupid person is of low disposition, and will have no faith in my magnificence, nor believe that I am his father. Under these circumstances, he orders persons of low character— crooked, one-eyed, maimed, ill-clad, and blackish — to go and search that man who shall do menial work, "Enter my service, and cleanse the putrid heap of dirt ; I will give thee a

way off, his father saw him, and had compassion, and ran, and fell on his neck, and kissed him. And the son said unto him, Father, I have sinned against heaven, and in thy sight, and am no more worthy to be called thy son. But the father said to his servants, Bring forth the best robe, and put it on him ; and put a ring on his hand, and shoes on his feet; and bring hither the fatted calf, and kill it ; and let us eat and be merry ; for this my son was dead, and is alive again ; he was lost, and is found."

double salary" (are the words of the message). On hearing this call, the poor man comes and cleanses the said spot ; he takes up his abode there in a hovel near the mansion. . . Little by little he makes the man enter the house, and employs him in his service for fully twenty years, in the course of which time he succeeds in inspiring him with confidence. At the same time he lays up in the house, gold, pearls, crystal. . . The ignorant man, who is living outside the mansion, alone in a hovel, cherishes no other ideas but of poverty, and thinks to himself : Mine are no such possessions. The rich man perceiving this of him (thinks) : My son has arrived at the consciousness of being noble. He calls together a gathering of his friends and relatives (and says) : I will give all my property to this man. In the midst of the assembly, where the king, burghers, citizens, and many mer-

chants were present, he
speaks thus : This is my
son whom I lost a long time
ago. It is now fully fifty
years — and twenty years
more during which I have
seen him—that he disap-
peared from such and such
a place, and that in his
search I came to this place.
He is owner of all my property ; to him I leave it all
and entirely ; let him do
with it what he wants. I
give him my whole family
property. And the (poor)
man is struck with surprise ;
remembering his former
poverty, his low disposition
[or, position] and as he receives those good things of
his father's and the family
property, he thinks, Now
am I a happy man.

In like manner has the
leader, who knows our low
disposition (or, position), not
declared to us, "Ye shall
become Buddhas ;" but
"Ye are, certainly, my disciples and sons."

v. 44. As the light of the
sun and moon, Kasyapa
shines upon all the world ;

St. Matt. v. 45, 48, "He
maketh His sun to rise on
the evil and on the good,

upon the virtuous and the wicked : upon high and low . . as their beams are sent down upon everything equally, without inequality (partiality) ; so too . . . the preaching of the true law proceeds equally in respect to all beings.

and sendeth rain on the just, and on the unjust. Be ye therefore perfect, even as your Father which is in heaven is perfect."

It is as if a potter made different vessels out of the same clay. Some of these pots are to contain sugar ; others ghee ; others curds and milk ; others of inferior quality are vessels of impurity. There is no diversity in the clay used ; no, the diversity of the pots is only due to the substances which are put into each of them.

Romans ix. 21, "Hath not the potter power over the clay, of the same lump to make one vessel unto honour, and another unto dishonour ?"

xii. 15. I do not care for my body or life, O Lord ; but as keepers of thine entrusted deposit, we care for enlightenment.

Acts xx. 24, "Neither count I my life dear unto myself, so that I might finish my course with joy, and the ministry which I have received of the Lord Jesus."

xii. 16. The Lord Himself knows that in the last period there are (to be) wicked monks who do not understand mysterious speech.

2 Tim. iii. 1, "This know also that in the last days perilous times shall come." 1 Tim. iv. 1, "In the latter times some shall depart from the faith."

xii. 17. One will have to bear frowning looks, repeated disavowal (or concealment), expulsion from the monasteries, many and manifold abuses.

St. John xvi. 2, "They shall put you out of the synagogues; yea, the time cometh, that whosoever killeth you will think that he doeth God service."

The Questions of King Milinda.

iii. 6, 8. The king said, "Venerable Nâgasena, where does wisdom dwell?" "Nowhere, O king." "Then, Sir, there is no such thing as wisdom." "Where does the wind dwell, O king?" "Not anywhere, Sir." "Then, there is no such thing as wind." "Well answered, Nâgasena."

Job xxviii. 12-14, "But where shall wisdom be found? And where is the place of understanding? Man knoweth not the price thereof; neither is it found in the land of the living. The deep saith, It is not in me; And the sea saith, It is not with me."

iii. 7, 2. The king said, "Your people say, Nâgasena, that though a man should have lived a hundred years an evil life, yet if, at the moment of death, thoughts of the Buddha should enter his mind, he will be reborn among the gods."

St. Luke xxiii. 42, 43, "And he said, Jesus, remember me when Thou comest in Thy kingdom, And He said unto him, Verily, I say unto thee, to-day shalt thou be with Me in Paradise."

The Lalita Vistara.

xiii. 12. Pour forth for the world the ever-flowing water of the river of the Law.

St. John iv. 14, "The water that I shall give him shall be in him a well of

17. After having attained the dignity of a Buddha free from death, free from grief, I shall satisfy with deathlessness, those whom thirst consumes.

water springing up unto eternal life."

Rev. xxi. 6, " I will give unto him that is athirst of the fountain of the water of life freely."

18. For the ignorant who are in the path of doubt cause the pure bright light of wisdom to shine.

St. John viii. 12, " He that followeth Me shall not walk in darkness, but shall have the light of life."

143. He who is bound, cannot set another free : a blind man cannot point out the way.

St. Luke vi. 39, " Can the blind guide the blind ? Shall they not both fall into a pit ? "

The Abhinishkramana Sûtra.

iii. Though the heavens were to fall to earth, and the great world be swallowed up and pass away ; though Mount Sumeru were to crack in pieces, and the great ocean be dried up, yet, Ananda, be assured the words of the Buddha are true. — BEAL'S *Romantic Legend.*

St. Matt. xxiv. 35, " Heaven and earth shall pass away, but My words shall not pass away."

Wisudhi-Margga-sanné.

It is better to have a redhot piece of iron run through the eye, than for the eye to

St. Matt. xviii. 9, " And if thine eye causeth thee to stumble, pluck it out and

be permitted to wander, as
by this means evil desire
will be produced.—SPENCE
HARDY'S *Manual of Bud-
dhism.*

cast it from thee ; it is good
for thee to enter into life
with one eye, rather than
having two eyes to be cast
into the hell of fire."

2. *Points of contact and of contrast in Christian and Buddhist teaching.*

In order to form a just estimate of the possible influence of Buddhism upon primitive Christianity, it is
necessary to take account of evidence other than that of
isolated passages such as have been given in the list.
There are truths taught alike by both systems ; there are
also important differences upon subjects that belong to
the essence of religion. The weight of evidence can
best be tested by placing side by side the features of
resemblance and of difference. In some cases it is not
easy to draw the line between points of contact and of
contrast; for where there is identity of subject matter,
coupled with divergence of treatment, likeness and
unlikeness strangely co-mingle.

A. CONTACT.

Christianity and Buddhism to a large extent agree in
the following respects :—

(1) *The Nature of Righteousness.* Preceding systems
had in both cases laid an undue stress upon ritual ; in
contrast with this, righteousness is made a matter not of
ceremonial observance but of the inner life. When
external rites are given a predominant importance, they

become worse than useless ; they lead to self-deception, to unreality, to a low moral standard ; the cleansing of the heart must take precedence of every other effort in the attainment of righteousness.

(2) *The Importance of Righteousness.* It is supreme, so that, in contrast with it, worldly advantages are as nothing ; for it men may safely and wisely part with everything else ; whatever comes between them and it must be got rid of, no matter how dear the hindrance may be, no half measures will suffice ; he who seeks righteousness must seek it with his whole heart ; the desire for righteousness is the noblest aspiration of the human heart.

(3) *The Nature of Sin.* It comes from within ; its root and not its fruit merely must be got rid of ; it looks attractive, but it invariably brings sorrow in its train ; it is insidious in its growth ; steadfast effort is necessary in order to overcome it.

(4) *The World.* It is full of dangers and temptations, of snares and pitfalls for the unwary. Its pleasures are enticing, but they promise more than they can afford in the way of gratification ; they are at best shortlived and unsatisfying ; they are often utterly delusive, so that men make a great sacrifice to obtain what proves only a source of trouble. There are many sorrows in the world, from which there is no escape ; such uncertainty, that no human being can count on anything he holds dear being left to him for a single day. The wise will not allow their hearts to be enchained by the seductions of the world ; they will choose what is enduring rather than what is transient—what is sure rather than what is changeful and impermanent.

(5) *The Path of Duty.* It is difficult, so that, comparatively speaking, few tread it ; it requires the whole-hearted

effort of a resolute mind to enter it ; and, having entered
it, to persevere to the end.

(6) *A Man's Work begins with Himself.* The faults of
others are more easily perceived, and can be readily
condemned ; but it is hopeless, so far as success is concerned, and useless for the man himself, to reprove others
for what he permits in his own case.

(7) *The Duties of Life.* A man must govern himself and
keep his body under control ; he must strive after
purity—purity of heart as well as of life ; he must be
absolutely truthful ; he must live in concord and harmony, as far as possible, with all men, specially with
those who are bound to him by the tie of a common
faith ; he must rule his tongue, and abstain from all
hurtful and unkind words as well as acts ; he must be
active and diligent, turning his life to the best possible
account ; he must be humble and lowly, contented with
such things as he has.

(8) *The Personal Founder*, but with the difference that
has been pointed out—namely, that to the early Christians
it was Christ Himself, His Personal Life and Work,
that held the foremost place ; in the case of the early
Buddhists it was Gautama's teaching that was regarded
as of primary importance.

(9) *The Visible Society* as the means of preserving and
propagating the tenets of the Founder.

B. CONTRAST.

Christianity and Buddhism differ in the following
important respects :—

(1) Christ came to give new life to the world ; life
which was to endure for ever, over which death had no
power. Gautama taught the cessation of existence to be
the highest bliss.

(2) Christ taught self-surrender, as the highest act of a being endowed with free-will, to One infinitely wiser and better than man himself. Gautama taught self-reliance and self-sufficiency as characteristics of the greatest saints.

(3) Christ taught that in a life of absolute dependence upon God, men would attain holiness, as they received what they did not possess. Gautama taught absolute independence as essential for all who trode the path of righteousness.

(4) Christ taught the Fatherhood of God as the first of all truths. Gautama taught that, practically at least, there is no God, since man knows and can know nothing of Him if He does exist.

(5) Christ taught men, while mortifying their evil passions, to reverence their body as being the Temple of the Holy Ghost. Gautama taught men that the body is a seething mass of corruption and defilement.

(6) Christ taught men to consecrate their emotions and affections by loving God with all their heart, and their neighbour as themselves. Gautama taught men to crush their emotions and affections until they had reduced themselves to a state of absolute apathy.

(7) Christ taught men that family life was a Divine Ordinance, and a type of God's own relationship to the world. Gautama taught men that family life was an injurious fetter which the wise man will do well to sever.

(8) Christ taught men to look forward to a future state where their nature would be glorified, and their whole being fully developed. Gautama taught that any aspiration after a future life was a sign of imperfection, and a desire which must be quenched.

3. *The supposed influence of Buddhism upon early Christianity.*

The decision as to the influence of Buddhist conceptions upon primitive Christian teaching depends to some extent upon the evidence as to the spread of Buddhism to Palestine prior to the time of our Lord. It is important to emphasize the fact that from the Christian standpoint this question can be investigated with an unbiassed judgment. If Christ had found Buddhist conceptions prevalent amongst the Jews, it is beyond doubt that He would have incorporated into His teaching whatever of Light and Truth was contained in the great religion of the East. When He compares His kingdom to leaven, He directs attention to this special characteristic of assimilation which Christianity possesses. And we can judge, by His attitude towards contemporary Jewish conceptions and ceremonies, that He would have acted similarly in regard to the moral teaching of Buddhism. St. Paul, by his quotations from Heathen writers, and by the use which he makes of Stoic thought in speaking to the Athenians, gives proof of his readiness to avail himself of truth, wheresoever it was to be found. There is, therefore, no need to dismiss on *à priori* grounds the possibility that Buddhist teaching was adopted into the primitive Christian faith. The question must be decided by evidence—the external evidence of the spread of Buddhism, and the internal evidence derived from a comparison of the two systems.

The passage in the Mahâva*m*sa which relates that at the dedication of the Buddhist Tope in B.C. 167 "thirty thousands priests from Alasaddá, the capital of the Yoná country attended," was quoted by Hilgenfeld and others as a proof of the early spread of Buddhism to the far West, for they identified Alasaddá with Alexandria in

Egypt. Bishop Lightfoot pointed out that this supposition was exceedingly improbable (Commentary on the Epistle to the Colossians, p. 152) ; and Turnour, in his translation of the Mahâvamsa, suggested that Yoná was a division of India not identified. Bearing in mind the number of cities then called Alexandria, the question of determining which was intended might seem only a matter of conjecture. But in "The Questions of King Milinda" evidence is supplied which seems to put an end to the difficulty, "The Elder replied, 'In what district, O king, were you born?' 'There is an island called Alasanda ; it was there I was born.' 'And how far is Alasanda from here?' 'About two hundred leagues.'" (Sacred Books of the East, vol. xxxv., p. 127). This Alexandria, Prof. Rhys Davids points out, was in Baktria, and was the name either of a city, or more probably of an Island, in the Indus, on which the city Kalasi was built (ib., preface, p. xxiii.). The whole evidence is in favour of the identification of this Alexandria in Baktria with the Alasaddá of the Yoná country mentioned in the Mahâvamsa.

The inscriptions of King Asoka supply stronger testimony. Asoka was grandson of Chandragupta, called by the Greeks Sandrakottus, the ally of Seleukos Nicator. He reigned from B.C. 260 to 223 ; and his inscriptions on rocks, in caves, and on pillars, furnish most important testimony as to early Buddhism. One of the Rock inscriptions runs thus :—"Everywhere within the conquered province of Raja Piyadasi [that is 'the humane' ; it is the name given to Asoka in the inscriptions]—the beloved of the gods, as well as in the parts occupied by the faithful, such as Chola, Pida, Satiyaputra, and Ketalaputra, even as far as Tambapamû [Ceylon] ; and, moreover, within the dominions of Antiochus, the Greek

(of which Antiochus' generals are the rulers), everywhere
the heaven-beloved Raja Piyadasi's double system of
medical aid is established, both medical aid for men and
medical aid for animals, together with the medicaments
of all sorts, which are suitable for men and suitable for
animals" (Cunningham's Corpus Inscriptionum Indicarum, Rock Inscriptions, Edict ii.).   The edicts mention
not only Antiochus (that is Antiochus Theos of Syria),
but also Ptolemy Philadelphus of Egypt; Antigonus
Gonnatas of Macedonia ; Magas of Cyrene, and
Alexander II. of Epirus.   Thus it is possible that the
inscriptions indicate a greater knowledge of the western
world, and consequently a more frequent communication
with it, than some writers have supposed.   Hence Dr.
Mahaffy concludes, "We may take it as probable that
Buddhist missionaries preached in Syria two centuries
before the teaching of Christ (which has so many moral
points in common) was heard in Northern Palestine." He
adds, "So true is it that every great historical change has
had its forerunner, and that people's minds must be
gradually led to the great new truths, which are indeed the
gift of Divine inspiration" (*Alexander's Empire*, p. 140).
It must, however, be borne in mind that the statements
made in the inscriptions are exceedingly vague ; it is
quite impossible to determine the amount of real acquaintanceship with the West that underlies the mention of
these names, and how far they can be taken as indi-
cating a spread of Buddhism to Palestine in the second
century B.C.

It seems to me that although they would furnish very
important subsidiary evidence, the testimony of the inscriptions by itself is insufficient, and that its validity
must be tested by a consideration of what may be urged
upon the other side.

Now there are two facts that have to be borne in mind as testifying against the theory that Buddhism had spread thus far west as this early date. The first is the absence of any indications, outside the Inscriptions of Asoka, that India and Western Asia were in communication with each other at that period; and secondly the absence in early Christian writers of any allusion to Buddhism, or of any acquaintance with its tenets: "Clement of Alexandria, writing in the latest years of the second century or the earliest of the third, for the first time mentions Buddha by name; and even he betrays a strange ignorance of this Eastern religion" (Lightfoot, *Colossians*, p. 155). It is difficult to reconcile specially this latter fact with such a diffusion of Buddhist thought in Palestine as would have made it a forerunner of Christianity.

I have said so far nothing of the Essenes, who have been described as Buddhist Jews. Bishop Lightfoot discusses their doctrines and practices in detail, and his conclusion is that the foreign element in Essenism was derived from the Zoroastrian religion (*Colossians*, p. 151), and Edersheim, in his "Life and Times of Jesus the Messiah," concurs in this view. But I do not think there is anything that has been written on this subject that is as forcible as Dr. Ginsburg's article on "The Essenes" in Smith's *Dictionary of Christian Biography*. He argues very conclusively that there was no foreign element in Essenism; that the sect sprang from what the Talmud calls the seventh kind of Pharisee — namely, the *Pharisee from love*, who is one from pure love to God; and that the supposed antipathy of the Essenes to sacrifice and their sun worship are founded upon a complete misunderstanding of their beliefs and practices. We can thus understand why they are not distinctly mentioned

in the New Testament ; they are classed together with
the other divisions of the sect under the common title of
Pharisees. It does not appear, therefore, that they enter
into this argument, whatever points of similarity exist
between Essenism and Buddhism are points in which all
ascetic systems are at one.

Turning to internal evidence, I must refer first of all
to the list of parallel passages given in the beginning of
this Appendix. The value of the list consists in this,
that it shows how hazardous a course it is to found an
argument upon coincidences of thought or of expression.
It seems to me that the parallelisms between the Book
of Proverbs and the Buddhist Books are quite as striking
as those between the Buddhist Books and the New
Testament Scriptures. If the list is studied, I believe
that the conclusion that will present itself to most minds
is that there is not a single passage that suggests the
idea that the one religion borrowed from the other. And
if parallelisms of thought and teaching are urged, it must
be remembered both that there are contrasts as well as
similarities, and also that it is in the enunciation of
moral duties that we may most surely trace the universal
diffusion of Divine light.

The points of contact between Christian and Buddhist
teaching explain themselves, to my mind, most reasonably
in this way. From a consideration of all the evidence, I
cannot come to the conclusion that Buddhism in any way
affected primitive Christian teaching. If either the external or the internal evidence was stronger, the contrary
position might be maintained. If in course of time fresh
testimony is forthcoming in support of the spread of
Buddhism to Palestine prior to the Christian era, then
we may have to re-examine the internal evidence, so as

to decide, in view of the increased evidence from external sources, whether our Scriptures do not themselves bear witness to Buddhist influence.

But while the testimony remains as it is at present, I can see no valid reason for doubting that the two religions are absolutely independent of one another.

4. *Buddhism and the Canonical Gospels.*

Reference has been made in Lecture VI. to the theory that the legendary life of Gautama affected the records of the Evangelists. The statements of writers who argue in favour of this or some kindred idea, are characterized by modes of argument which it would not be easy to parallel. It is said, for example, that "there can be hardly any doubt that Jesus of Nazareth, whose doctrines in their most essential parts are identical with those of the Buddha, must have been a disciple of Buddhist Mendicants from the age of twelve to thirty, a space totally unaccounted for by the Gospels, and that under their guidance he must have attained Arahatship. Later on He returned to his native country to preach the doctrine to his people" (*A Buddhist Catechism*, by Subhâdra Bhikshu, p. 80).

In a work entitled " *The Angel-Messiah of Buddhists, Essenes, and Christians*," by Ernest De Bunsen, an elaborate attempt is made to trace almost every dogma of Christianity back to a Buddhist source. But the nature of the evidence and the modes of argument that are adopted may be judged by the following extracts :—
" The doctrines of Gautama-Buddha centred in the belief of a personal God, and in man's continued existence after death " (p. 48). "The name Pythagoras appears

P

to be a combination of Put, Bud, Bod, or Bodhi, and
of 'Guru,' which word in India was used for a teacher
of the Veda; so that the name Pythagoras may be
interpreted 'Teacher of the religion of Buddha'" (p. 75).
"The name [Pharisees] having possibly been derived
from Pharis (Faris), the Arabian name for the Persians.
Comp. Phares and Pharesites, or Pheresites (Perizzites).
Phares was the son of a mixed marriage, which by a
figurative interpretation may have been referred to the
union of Hebrews and Kenites in Arad" (p. 86).

Statements scarcely less strange are to be found in
Lillie's *Buddhism in Christianity*. We are told that the
circumcision of Christ took place in the Temple at
Jerusalem according to the Canonical Gospels, and that
the giving of a name at circumcision was not a Jewish
custom (p. 22); that *Zacchæus* sat under his fig-tree (p. 121);
that Maranatha means "The Lord is *risen*" (p. 252).

Prof. Seydel is not guilty of such absurdities as these,
but his arguments for the influence of Buddhist legends
on the New Testament records of the life of Christ seem
a signal illustration of the number of proofs which an
ingenious mind can discover in support of any position,
no matter how apparently untenable. From first to last
it is a case of special pleading, and it is quite possible, in
many instances, to make a retort, and to use what Seydel
quotes to prove that Christianity has borrowed from
Buddhism, as an argument that Buddhism has availed
itself of our Scriptures. For example, when the fact of
St. John recording that our Lord saw Nathanael under
the fig-tree is brought forward to show that the Evangelist
was influenced by the reminiscence of Gautama sitting
under the fig-tree, we cannot but feel that there is much
more to be said in support of Bishop Bigandet's idea
that the Bo-tree, or tree of knowledge, is a relic of the

primeval traditions of Paradise contained in the Book of Genesis (*Life or Legend of Gaudama*. This book being out of print, I have been obliged to use the French translation of it, by Victor Gauvain ; the passage referred to runs as follows : " Si l'on se remet en mémoire les cas nombreux et frappants de certains faits, certaines vérités révélées, offerts à l'attention du lecteur de cette légende, sous une forme défigurée, mais encore reconnaissable, on se trouve alors conduit tout simplement, et avec toutes chances de vraisemblance, à supposer qu'il y a de plus en ceci un reflet de la tradition de l'arbre de la science, qui occupait le centre du jardin d'Eden," p. 90). Those who reject Bigandet's view as untenable have far more cause to regard Seydel's idea as absurd.

Again, when Seydel urges every point of contact between Buddhism and Christianity as evidencing that the latter religion was directly influenced by the former, it is not surprising that some writers reverse the position, and maintain that the later Buddhist Legends show signs of acquaintanceship with the Gospel History. Thus the late Prof. Beal, in his " *Buddhist Literature in China*," says : "Altogether, having translated the Buddhacharita throughout, and also the greater portion of Asvaghosha's Sermons, I am impressed with the conviction that Christian teaching had reached his ears at the time when Asvaghosha was in Parthia, or at any rate in Bactria (viz, about A.D. 70), and that he was influenced by it so far as to introduce into Buddhism the changes we find beginning to take shape at this period. The doctrine of a universal salvation, and of Buddha's incarnation by the descent of the Spirit, and by a power of Bodhi, or wisdom, by which we are made sons or disciples—these and other non-Buddhist ideas found in Asvaghosha's writings, convince me that there was such an intercommunication

at this time between East and West as shaped the later
school of Buddhism into a pseudo-Christian form ; and
this accounts very much for some other inexplicable similarities" (Introduction, p. xiv.).

It may be worth while to quote here one or two illustrations from the sermons of Asvaghosha where they run
on New Testament lines : "Come, now, I will use a
comparison to illustrate this argument.   It is like a grain
of corn ; when all concomitant circumstances are in
suitable relation, then the blade is produced; but in
truth it is not *this grain* which produces the blade, for
the grain dies (in the ground) ; the new blade grows and
increases, but the old grain perishes ; because *it* dies *the*
blade lives, the two cannot be separated.   So it is Buddha
speaks with respect to the future body" (p. 119).   "Have
you not rather heard what Tathágata says in the Sûtra
(where he bids his followers) not to despise the little
child called 'Snake-fire'?   So neither should we despise
the young Shamis" (p. 122).

In estimating the significance of the points of similarity, given by Seydel, it is important to bear in mind
that a very large number of the parallelisms he alleges
are drawn from Buddhist Legends, which date subsequently to the Christian era.   And as a general answer
to his main argument that Buddhist Legend influenced
the Gospel Records, three facts are important.   (1) From
the standpoint of literary criticism, the Gospels bear no
evidence of being pieces of patchwork made up of
materials drawn from different and dissimilar sources.
(2) The interval of time between the Life of our Lord
and the publication of the Gospels was wholly insufficient
for such a process as Seydel's theory necessitates.   The
same argument that broke down Strauss' "Mythical
Theory," applies with equal force to Seydel's view.

(3) The story of Barlaam and Joasaph supplies a case in point in which Buddhist Legend is interwoven with a supposed life of a Christian saint. We can judge to some extent by this parallel what our Gospels would have been if what Seydel alleges had really taken place.

It is most satisfactory to be able to quote Prof. Rhys Davids on the subject of the influence of Buddhism on the New Testament. He says : " It is true that many passages in these two literatures can be easily shown to have a similar tendency. But when some writers on the basis of such similarities proceed to argue that there must have been some historical connection between the two, and that the New Testament, as the later, must be the borrower, I venture to think that they are wrong. There does not seem to me to be the slightest evidence of any historical connection between them ; and whenever the resemblance is a real one—and it often turns out to be really least when it first seems to be greatest, and really greatest when it first seems least—it is due, not to any borrowing on the one side or on the other, but solely to the similarity of the conditions under which the two movements grew." He adds, when it is concluded that the parallels are " an unanswerable indication of the obligations of the New Testament to Buddhism, I must ask to be allowed to enter a protest against an inference which seems to me to be against the rules of sound historical criticism" (Introduction to Tevigga-Sutta, *Sacred Books of the East*, Vol. xi. p. 165).

5. *Similarity between Christian and Buddhist Asceticism.*

As a closing section in this Appendix, I add some extracts from books which represent ascetic Christianity ;

not that there is any likelihood that in this case, Buddhism exercised a direct influence, but in order to illustrate how similar the language of asceticism always is, even under variant conditions.

The following passages are from the " De Imitatione Christi," of St Thomas à Kempis.

I. xvii. 2. Wearing a dress and tonsure profit little ; but change of heart and perfect mortification of the passions make a truly religious man.

I. xxi. 1. It is a wonder that any man can ever perfectly rejoice in this life if he duly consider and thoroughly weigh his state of banishment and the many perils with which his soul is environed. Through levity of heart and small care for our failings, we feel not the real sorrows of our souls ; and so oftentimes we vainly laugh when we have just cause to weep.

I. xxii. 2. Truly it is misery even to live upon the earth. The more spiritual a man desires to be, the more bitter does this present life become to him ; because he sees more clearly and perceives more sensibly the defects of human corruption. For to eat and to drink, to sleep and to watch, to labour and to rest, and to be subject to other necessities of nature, is doubtless a great misery and affliction to a religious man, who would gladly be set loose and freed from all sin.

I. xxii. 5. So long as we carry about us this frail body of ours, we can never be without sin, nor live without weariness and pain.

III. xxvii. 1. According to the love and affection thou bearest to anything, so doth it cleave unto thee more or less.

The following quotations are from the writings of Miguel Molinos, the Quietist :—

" By not speaking, nor desiring, and not thinking, one arrives at the true and perfect mystical silence, wherein

God speaks with the soul, communicates Himself to it, and, in the abyss of its own depth, teaches it the most perfect and exalted wisdom."

"All these are effects of self-love, and if they be not denied it is impossible that a man should ever get up to the height of perfect contemplation, to the highest happiness of the loving union and lofty throne of peace internal."

"Look at *nothing*, desire *nothing*, will *nothing*, endeavour *nothing*; and then *in everything* thy soul will live reposed with quiet and enjoyment. This is the way to get purity of soul, perfect contemplation, and peace internal. Walk, therefore, in this safe path, and endeavour to overwhelm thyself in this *nothing*; endeavour to use thyself to sink deep into it, if thou hast a mind to be annihilated, united, and transformed."

APPENDIX III.

NIRVÂNA.

IN endeavouring to arrive at the signification given to Nirvâna by Gautama, it is well to trace back the meaning of the term, so as to see the modifications it has undergone in course of time.

We begin therefore with the Buddhists of our own day. What do they understand by Nirvâna?

In Olcott's *Buddhist Catechism*, Nirvâna is defined to be "A condition of total cessation of changes, of perfect rest; of the absence of desire, and illusion, and sorrow; of the total obliteration of everything that goes to make up the physical man. Before reaching Nirvâna, man is constantly being reborn; when he reaches Nirvâna, he is reborn no more" (p. 13).

Subhádra Bhikshu, in his Catechism, gives a somewhat similar definition. "It (Nirvâna) is a condition of heart and mind, in which every earthly craving is extinct ; it is the cessation of every passion and desire, of every feeling of ill-will, fear, and sorrow. It is a mental state of perfect rest and peace and joy, in the steadfast assurance of deliverance attained, from all the imperfections of finite being. It is a condition impossible to be defined in words, or to be conceived by any one still attached to the things of the world. Only he knows what Nirvâna is who has realized it in his own heart" (p. 39). He further states in a note, "Nirvâna signifies a state of supreme moral perfection impossible to be conceived by any one who still wears the fetters of earthly desires. . . Parinirvâna, in the sense of other religions and of scientific materialism, does certainly mean "annihilation"; for nothing whatever remains of the constituents of human life. But from the point of view taken by the Arahat, it is the world, with all its appearances, that is nought, is illusion, error ; whilst Parinirvâna is the entering into eternity ; the everlasting true existence, where all suffering, individuality, separate being, and transmigration are at an end" (pp. 83, 84). Both these writers represent the views of the Southern Buddhists.

In a paper on "*The Nirvâna of the Northern Buddhists*," Dr. Edkins treats of the present ideas of the Chinese Buddhists on this subject. He says, "The usual translation of the Sanskrit word 'Nirvâna,' in the Chinese translations, is *mie tu*, 'destruction and salvation.' The idea is that salvation is found in extinction. Death is viewed as a glorification. . . It is the triumph of the ascetic life over the body. The body, says the Buddhist, is impregnated with the principles of evil, and in the Nirvâna evil is finally conquered. . . Belief in the Nirvâna seems to be the assurance felt that

in death the highest possible condition of the soul is
attained. . . In the Nirvâna there is no life, no death,
no present, no future. . . Consciousness must not be
predicated of the soul, nor must the soul be imagined as
having individual existence, or any realized independent
life" (p. 7). "On the whole, it may be said, respecting
the views held on the Nirvâna by the Northern Buddhists, that they comprehend all varieties. They have a
popular teaching and a higher gnosis. They teach the
metempsychosis, but they do not insist on it. If it suits
your state of mind, well. They will show you how, by
Buddha's wisdom, you may reach the final escape from
the delusion of existence in which you are enthralled,
and, leaving the sea of misery, arrive at the Nirvâna's
peaceful shore. The means are found in moral reformation and contemplative devotion. But if you are sceptical,
they have a higher gnosis, the Mahayana. You must
submit to a pitiless argument, to prove that nothing
exists which men think exists, and that annihilation is
desirable. You must learn to look on life itself as painful.
The moral feelings and convictions are founded on an in-
tellectual weakness. Love, piety, and benevolence are but
delusive elements in the great delusive whole, to which the
unenlightened at present belong. In proportion, as you
recognize this, do you approximate to the Nirvâna, for in
that there is no distinction of life and death, or of good and
evil. But then comes again the inextinguishable consciousness of future existence. The disciple will not be
content with this pitiless logic, and the Mahayana finds for
him a suitable doctrine, that of the Western Paradise. The
Buddhist teacher will not allow that imperfection exists
in Buddha's teaching. Those who long for heaven have
a heaven provided for them. This is, however, only a
means to an end. The higher gnosis knows only annihilation, and bases it only on what is held by its advo-

cates to be metaphysical necessity. Should another objector appear and say that the Nirvâna is attainable now, and that not only did Buddha himself reach this state, but that all those who give themselves to a life of pure devotion and fixed contemplation may attain it— the upholders of the Mahàyana consent to this, but add that it is merely a temporary and limited Nirvâna, which is preliminary to that which they hold to be final" (pp. 20, 21).

In Alabaster's *Wheel of the Law*, it is said that the Siamese always refer to it (Nirvâna) as something existing, as in the phrases : " Nirvâna is a place of comfort where there is no care ; lovely is the glorious realm of Nirvâna" (Note 6 on *Life of Buddha*).

There would appear, therefore, at present to be three meanings assigned to the term Nirvâna, by members of the Buddhist community. Some regard it as a future state of existence, free from sorrow, from care, from strife, from death ; where there is calm, peace, and joy. Others who are more deeply imbued with the tenets of the system, and who view sorrow and existence as inseparable, interpret Nirvâna as annihilation. While Buddhists, who are of a metaphysical type of mind, conceive Nirvâna to be a kind of unconscious existence, in which all that appertains to physical life has vanished. The soul that has battled against and vanquished desire, attains its ideal in which it knows nothing, feels nothing— in some senses, is nothing.

In determining which of these three views most closely represents the idea of Nirvâna as taught by Gautama, we may at once put the first view aside. Those who regard Nirvâna as a future state of existence in which there will be consciousness and individual life absolutely oppose one of the fundamental points of Gautama's teaching.

However he might have conceded such a mode of existence to be a preparation for Nirvâna, there is no doubt that he would have declined to accept this definition as describing Nirvâna in the true sense of the term. The intrusion of such a conception into Buddhism seems to owe its origin to an alteration that took place in regard to the continued existence of the Buddha. The Canonical Sacred Books taught that he died and passed away. "When the stalk to which a bunch of mangos is united is cut off, all the mangos united to that stalk accompany it ; even so, priests, the body of Tathágata, whose stalk of existence is entirely cut off, still remains ; and so long as that body remains, he will be seen by gods and men ; but upon the termination of life, when the body is broken up, gods and men shall not see him" (*Brahmajâla Sutta*, quoted by D'Alwis, Nirvâna, p. 51).

But in the Legends a different idea is suggested. Max Müller speaks of the appearances of the Buddha to his disciples after his death as one argument against Nirvâna signifying annihilation (Preface to *Buddha-gosha's Parables*, p. xli.). The origin of the idea may be traced back to the reverence done to the relics of Gautama (*Mahâ-parinibbâna-sutta*, vi. 51-63). And in "*The Questions of King Milinda*," one of the dilemmas proposed by the king is, "If the Buddha accepts gifts he cannot have entirely passed away. . . . On the other hand, if he be entirely passed away (from life), un-attached to the world, escaped from all existence, then honours would not be offered to him." Nâgasena replied, "The Blessed One, O king, is entirely set free. And the Blessed One accepts no gift. Even at the foot of the Tree of Wisdom he abandoned all accepting of gifts ; how much more then, now, when he has passed entirely away by that kind of passing away which leaves no root over (for the formation of a new existence)."

Nâgasena then reconciles this idea with the offering of gifts : " If gods or men put up a building to contain the jewel treasure of the relics of a Tathâgata who does not accept their gift, still by that homage paid to the attainment of the supreme good under the form of the jewel treasure of his wisdom do they themselves attain to one or other of the three glorious states." Illustrations are added which show how completely Nâgasena believed the Buddha to have passed away. He is compared to a fire that has gone out ; to a wind that has ceased to blow ; to the sound of a drum that has died away. It is emphatically stated that the Buddha neither knows nor acquiesces in the honours done to him ; their effect wholly concerns the persons who offer the gifts. The illustration is used of the earth which does not acquiesce in all kinds of seeds being planted in it, yet the seeds spring up and bear fruit. The conclusion is drawn : " Therefore is it, O king, that an act done to the Tathâgata, notwithstanding his having passed away and not consenting thereto, is nevertheless of value, and bears fruit" (*S. B. E.*, vol. xxxv., pp. 144-154).

In the Saddharma-pundarîka a different conception is presented ; but in dealing with its testimony it must be borne in mind that it is one of a class of Buddhist Books made up of different elements, and containing materials to which different dates must be assigned (*vide*, Kern's Introduction, p. xi. ; *S. B. E*, vol. xxi.) And the chapter on the " Duration of Life of the Tathâgata" contains ideas so apparently different from primitive Buddhism, that it would seem as if this part of the treatise must be of late date. The leading thought of the chapter is that the Tathâgata obtained enlightenment myriads of ages ago, but that he represented himself as only recently enlightened, "in order to lead creatures to full enlightenment and make them go in"; and that "the

Tathâgata, who so long ago was perfectly enlightened, is unlimited in the duration of his life, he is everlasting. Without being extinct, the Tathâgata makes a show of extinction, on behalf of those who have to be educated." The artifice thus practised is justified by an illustration. A physician has a number of sons ; on one occasion when he is absent from home they all incur a disease from poison, which causes severe pain, but manifests itself by different symptoms. On his return they requested a remedy ; he prepared one, and it was taken by those whose good sense remained. But some, whose ideas had become perverted by the disease, refused to partake of it. Thereupon the father determined to practise a device. He told them that he was very old ; that he was going away to die, but that he left the remedy so that they might partake of it, if they so willed. He then disappeared to another part of the country, and let his sick sons know that he was dead. They partook of the remedy, and when they were cured the physician returned. The illustration closes with the question, "Would any one charge that physician with falsehood on account of his using that device?" "No, certainly not." Some stanzas are added which assert the continued existence of the Buddha : "I show the place of extinction, I reveal to (all) beings a device to educate them ; albeit I do not become extinct at the time, and in this very place continue preaching the law. . . In the opinion that my body is completely extinct, they pay worship in many ways to the relics, but me they see not. They feel (however) a certain aspiration by which their mind becomes right. When such upright (or pious), mild, and gentle creatures leave off their bodies, I assemble the crowd of disciples and show myself here on the Gridhrakûta" (S. B. E., vol. xxi., p. 298-310).

It is evident on comparing this passage with the

quotation from "*The Questions of King Milinda*," that the Saddharma-puṇḍarîka represents a later development of Buddhist thought; and it further shows how the way was opened for an identification of Nirvâṇa with existence in the Fields of Glory. Not indeed that this idea of Nirvâṇa is taught in the Saddharma-puṇḍarîka; it merely laid the foundation on which the idea was afterwards built. For what it states is that the Buddha only *seemed* to enter Nirvâṇa; he did not in reality enter that state in its fulness. No statements could be found stronger than this Book contains as to what Nirvâṇa signifies: "To-day, O monks, this very night, in the middle watch, will the Tathâgata, by entering the element of absolute Nirvâṇa, become wholly extinct" (p. 22). "That very night, in the middle watch, he met complete extinction, like a lamp when the cause (of its burnings) is exhausted" (p. 27). "After having revealed perfect enlightenment and led many koṭis of beings to perfect rest, he himself will be extinguished like a lamp when the oil is exhausted" (p. 279).

Now if the signification of Nirvâṇa that would make it practically equivalent to "Future Life" be put aside as inconsistent with the teaching of primitive Buddhism, the decision as to its true meaning lies between regarding it as Annihilation Absolute and Annihilation Relative, between total extinction, and the extinction of the conditions and concomitants of physical life. To this latter meaning Colebrooke refers when he writes: "Nirvâṇa is perfect calm. In its ordinary signification, as an adjective, it signifies extinct as a fire which is gone out; set, as a luminary which has gone down; defunct, as a saint who has passed away. Its etymology is from *vâ*, to blow as wind, with the preposition *nir*, used in a negative sense; it means calm and unruffled. The notion which is attached to the word in the acceptation

now under consideration is that of perfect apathy. . .
It is not annihilation, but unceasing apathy, which they understand to be the extinction (Nirvâna) of their saints" (*Essays*, vol. ii., p. 425).

In deciding between these two significations of the term, we may start from what appears to be universally admitted, namely, that the third division of the Buddhist Canon, the Abhidhamma, attaches to Nirvâna the sense of annihilation. But Max Müller has argued (*a*) that the Abhidhamma is of inferior authority to the other divisions of the Canon ; and (*b*) that the testimony of the Suttas and the Vinaya is against this signification of the word. His conclusion is that annihilation was not the meaning given to Nirvâna by Gautama, but a later signification invented or adopted by his followers.

But in the Introduction to his translation of the Dhammapada in *The Sacred Books of the East*, Max Müller has himself stated that "We must always, I think, distinguish between the three portions of the Canon, called the basket of the Suttas, the basket of Vinaya, and the basket of Abhidhamma ; and the three subjects of Dhamma (Sutta), Vinaya, and Abhidhamma, treated in these baskets. The subjects existed, and were taught long before the baskets were definitely arranged. Dhamma had originally a much wider meaning than Sutta-piṭaka. It often means the whole teaching of Buddha ; and even when it refers more particularly to the Sutta-piṭaka, we know that the Dhamma there taught deals largely with Vinaya and Abhidhamma doctrines. Even the fact that at the First Council, according to the description given in the Kullavagga, the Vinaya and Dhamma only were rehearsed, though proving the absence at that time of the Abhidhamma as a separate Piṭaka, by no means excludes the subject of the Abhidhamma having been taught under the head of Dhamma" (*S. B. E.*, vol. x., p. xxxiii.).

D'Alwis asserts that Sutra or Sutta was the name given both to the Sutta and Abhidhamma divisions of the Canon as contra-distinguished from the Vinaya (Buddhist Nir-vâna, p. 28), which would account for no special mention of the rehearsal of the Abhidhamma at the First Council. But even granting fully all that Max Müller states, there are two facts that must be borne in mind—(*a*) that he admits that Abhidhamma *doctrines* were taught by Gautama, and (*b*) that he fixes the closing of the Buddhist Canon after the Second, and possibly at the Third Council (B.C. 242) ; while most of the books were included in the Canon as early as the Second Council (B.C. 377). Now as, according to Max Müller, the date of the death of Gautama is B.C. 477, the interval of time is short for the introduction of a new signification of a term which occupied so prominent a place in the system.

Granting, however, that it is an open question, whether in this particular the Abhidhamma teaches the views of Gautama or those only of his followers ; there are three further questions that have to be considered. (1) Does the existing evidence make it probable that an Annihila-tion theory was an invention of Buddhists after Gautama's time? (2) Is the teaching of the Sutta and Vinaya Pitakas on this matter at variance with that of the Abhidhamma? and (3) What is the testimony of the whole system of Buddhist teaching?

Now, as we follow down the course of Buddhist thought, the tendency is certainly not in the direction of Annihilation. The later Books and the Legends invent for Gautama a continued existence, a power of manifest-ing himself, of which the Canonical Books contain no traces. So, also, they speak of a life in the Fields of Glory for his disciples. Therefore, on this line of evidence it would appear as if the probabilities were against the idea of Annihilation as a development of thought subsequent to the days of Gautama. The tendencies are against, rather than in favour of, such a dogma.

But if it can be shown that the Sutta and Vinaya Piṭakas testify against Annihilation, the question is practically settled. That they do not testify against it is evident from the fact that no passage has been quoted from these divisions of the Canon that is at variance with the Annihilation theory. The doubt as to their evidence has arisen from the fact mentioned in Lecture IV., that Nirvâna has a double meaning, or, rather, that there are two degrees of Nirvâna. It is applied to the earthly life of the Arahat; he attains Nirvâna while his existence still continues, but at the close of the existence in which he attains the saintly state, he receives Nirvâna in its fulness. Childers discusses very fully the difficulty how the one term Nirvâna can be used in the apparently contradictory senses of "bliss, happiness, peace, and calm" on the one hand, and of "Annihilation" on the other. He explains this anomaly thus : (1) Arhatship and Annihilation of being are inextricably interwoven, neither being without the other. (2) Annihilation enters into both significations : Arhatship being the Annihilation of suffering, original sin, karma, of everything except the skandhas ; Nirvâna [in its full significance] being the Annihilation of every conceivable attribute of being. (3) Both can be equally spoken of as the reward of a virtuous life. (4) The tie that binds the Arhat to life is only the slender film of human life. (5) The Arhat so soon attains Nirvâna [in its fulness] that it may be spoken of as actually his (*Pali Dictionary*, s.v. Nibbānam).

It must, therefore, be remembered that the passages in the Sutta or Vinaya Piṭakas that apparently oppose

Annihilation as the signification of Nirvâ*n*a, do not really
bear that interpretation, inasmuch as they refer to the
Nirvâ*n*a of the present, the life of the Arahat, who has
entered the fourth stage of the Path, who has severed every
fetter, and who alone awaits the close of his present life to
receive the fulness of release—release from existence.

Further, there is direct evidence, from these divisions
of the Canon, in favour of Annihilation as the signification
of Nirvâ*n*a. Three striking illustrations of its meaning
are found, all pointing in the same direction : "Nirvâ*n*a
is compared to the 'blowing out of a fire' . . . in
the Ratana Sutta : 'Are there any whose old (kamma)
has been destroyed, in whom no new (kamma) has been
produced, and whose hearts no longer cleave to future
existence ; they (are such as) have destroyed the seed of
existence, and have no desire of birth. (Such) sensible
persons are extinguished (blown out) like this lamp.'
Nirvâ*n*a is again compared to the rootless trunk of a
Palmyra. Now, it is a remarkable fact that of all the
Palms, the Palmyra is one, if not the only one, of the
trees which can never be grown denuded of its roots.
We have seen instances of large Coco, Areka, and Kitul
trees being transplanted ; but the Tálá can never be
grown in the same way, even when planted with its roots.
When, however, the Tálá is once cut off from the *vatthu*,
which adheres to the ground, it dies, and can never be
regenerated. . . . The very Dhammapada has an
illustration of Nirvâ*n*a which is by no means less clear
than any of the preceding : 'If, like a shattered metal-
plate [gong], thou dost not cause to utter thyself, thou art
one who has reached Nirvâ*n*a. Then there is no noisy
clamour to thee.' The above does not convey, as indi-
cated by Max Müller, that Nirvâ*n*a is 'rest, quietness,
and absence of passion.' On the contrary, it implies the
utter destruction of being " (D'Alwis, *Buddhist Nirvâ*n*a*,

pp. 33-36). There do not, therefore, appear to be sufficient grounds for supposing that the Sutta and Vinaya Piṭakas teach a different idea of Nirvâṇa from that contained in the Abhidhamma.

The final question to be determined is, which idea harmonizes more closely with the general system taught by Gautama.

Human nature is said to consist of five elements (khandhas), viz., Rúpa, "form"; Vedaná, "sensation"; Saññá, "perception" ("abstract ideas," Rhys Davids); Sankhárá, "discrimination" ("tendencies or potentialities," Rhys Davids); Viññáṇa, "consciousness" ("thought, reason," Rhys Davids). Buddhism teaches that "when a man dies, the khandhas of which he is constituted perish, but by the force of his kamma a new set of khandhas instantly starts into existence, and a new being appears in another world, who, though possessing different khandhas and a different form, is in reality identical with the man who has just passed away, because his kamma is the same. Kamma, then, is the link that preserves the identity of a being through all the countless changes which it undergoes in its progress through Samsára (succession of births). Desire (tanhá) produces clinging to existence (upádána); kamma works through upádána. The latter is the immediate cause of renewed existence; the former, the abiding cause" (Childers' *Pali Dictionary*, s.v. Khando and Upādānam).

When a Buddhist attains Nirvâṇa, his karma is destroyed. Is there then any other link in his chain of existence that still remains, and needs to be severed? Does he, according to Buddhism, retain anything except his present set of Khandhas, which will be broken up when he dies?

M. Foucaux believes that there is still, according to Buddhist teaching, the *soul* left, and that it survives the

destruction of the body.   He writes : "Après avoir lu,
avec la plus grande attention, l'article *Sankharo* du
dictionnaire Pâli, au lieu d'être convaincu, j'arrive juste à
une conclusion contraire à celle qu'attendait E. Childers,
tout simplement parce que j'aurais dû dire *l'âme* [Attâ]
au lieu de *l'esprit* [Mano].   Voici pourquoi : Les traditions bouddiques du Nord et du Sud s'accordent pour
nous dire que le Bouddha, et, après lui, les bouddhistes
de tous les temps, ont tenu pour certain que les âmes
n'ont pas eu de commencement.   Il s'en suit que les âmes
n'étant le produit d'aucune cause ne font pas partie des
composés, puisque, c'est Childers lui-même qui le dit :
les composés sont tout ce qui est le produit d'une cause
(*Annales du Musée Guimet,* tome vi. ; *Lalita Vistara,*
Introduction p. xiii.).

It is impossible to read these words without seeing
that they are the result of the inordinate value which
M. Foucaux assigns to Buddhist Legends, and of his
desire to make the Lalita Vistara—which he dates as
far back as the first century of the Christian era—the
exponent of primitive Buddhist teaching.

For the Sutta Pi*t*aka teaches what is in direct opposition
to the theory maintained by M. Foucaux.   "Anatta*m*, the
absence of a soul or self as abiding principle, is one of
the three parts of Buddhist wisdom and of Buddhist
perception " (*S. B. E.*, vol xi., p. 294 : Comp. Sabbâsava
Sutta 9, *ibid,* p. 299).   D'Alwis quotes a passage from
the Sa*n*yutta Nikáya in the Sutta Pi*t*aka, in which it is
taught that the idea of the *atta,* or soul, forming one of
the elements of being, leads to the conclusion, "*I am*" ;
hence follows Avijja, or Ignorance ; "but the Ignorance
of the learned disciple of the Ariya [sanctified] is extinct.
He begets knowledge, and being free from his Ignorance,
and by promoting knowledge, has no notion of ' I am,'
or that ' this is I am,' etc." (Buddhist Nirvâ*n*a, pp. 72, 73).

Viññâna, or Consciousness, is regarded by Oldenburg (*Buddha*, p. 228) and Sir Monier Williams (*Buddhism*, p. 109), as, at least practically, a permanent element in human nature, according to Buddhist teaching ; but only in the successive existences of an individual who has not attained Nirvâna, and not as an element surviving the death of the Arahat.

It cannot be said that, independently of the Khandhas, there was taught to be an *ego*. An *ego* implies individual life, and the perception of non-individuality was one of the preliminary steps to the attainment of Nirvâna (Compare Maha-parinibbana-Sutta I. 10). And Sir Coomára Swámy, in his preface to the Sutta Nipâta, states that "What was mostly aimed at by Hindu sages was the destruction of the ego-individuality. So long as this was attained, it mattered not much whether it was due to absorption or annihilation. Human misery arose from the assumption that there was such a thing as 'I.' Destroy this, and release, or Nibbâna, was instantly attained."

It cannot be urged that Buddhism taught absorption ; therefore, in this case, the desired end could only be arrived at by Annihilation.

An illustration from "*The Questions of King Milinda*" tends to prove that Buddhism recognized no super-sensuous element which could survive the shock of death in the case of the Arahat. Nâgasena was asked his name by the king. He answered, but added that it was only "a designation in common use. For there is no permanent individuality (no soul) involved in the matter." The king next asked, if that were so, what was Nâgasena? and going through the different parts of the body and the five elements of being, inquired in regard to each if that was Nâgasena. When in every case the answer was "No"; he urged, "Then I can discover no Nâgasena. Nâgasena is a mere empty

sound." The elder replied by using the king's chariot
as an illustration ; and he inquired about each part, if
that was the chariot? And when he received to each
inquiry the answer, " No," he also drew the conclusion,
"Chariot is a mere empty sound." The king replied,
" It is on account of its having all these things—the
pole and the axle, the wheels and the framework, the
ropes, the yoke, the spokes, and the goad—that it comes
under the generally understood term, the designation in
common use of 'chariot.'" "Very good ! Your Majesty
has rightly grasped the meaning of 'chariot.' And just
even so it is on account of all those things you questioned
me about—the thirty-two kinds of organic matter in a
human body and the five constituent elements of being—
that I come under the generally understood term, the
designation in common use of 'Nâgasena.' For it was
said, Sire, by our Sister Va*g*irâ, in the presence of the
Blessed One : 'Just as it is by the condition precedent of the
co-existence of its various parts, that the word "chariot"
is used, just so it is that when the Skandhas are there,
we talk of a "being."'" (*S. B. E.*, vol. xxxv., p. 40-45).

The illustration suggests an absolutely materialistic
conception of human nature. And it is important to
notice that the quotation at the close of the extract is
from the Sa*m*yutta Nikâya, in the Sutta Pi*t*aka (see
Rhys Davids' Note *loc. cit.*).

If, then, Nirvâ*n*a be not Annihilation, which of the com-
ponent parts of human nature exists in that state ?

Oldenburg believes that primitive Buddhism evaded
the solution of this question : "Does the path lead into
a new existence? Does it lead into the Nothing? The
Buddhist creed rests in delicate equipoise between the
two. The longing of the heart that craves the eternal
has not nothing, and yet the thought has not a something, which it might firmly grasp" (*Buddha*, p. 284).

A review of the evidence suggests to my mind a different conclusion. Instead of "delicate equipoise," there appears a distinct inclination on the side of Annihilation.   There were certainly some questions which Gautama declined to answer, some problems which he declined to solve. But it was because he deemed their consideration "as worse than profitless, as the source of manifold delusions and superstitions." May we not add, because he felt also that such questions and problems vanished in the case of those who apprehended the full scope of his teaching?

APPENDIX IV.

BUDDHISM AND WOMEN.

THE absolute subordination of woman was a recognized principle of Buddhism.   If Gautama could have had his will, he would have allowed the members of the Order to have had nothing to do with them.   In "The Book of the Great Decease" the following dialogue is recorded : " How are we to conduct ourselves, Lord, with regard to womankind?"   " Don't see them, Ananda."   " But if we should see them, what are we to do?"   "Abstain from speech, Ananda."   " But if they should speak to us, Lord, what are we to do?"   "Keep wide awake, Ananda" (*S. B. E.*, vol. xi., p. 91).

Allusion has been made in Lecture II. to Gautama's reluctance to found an Order of female Mendicants ; the circumstances are given in detail in the Sacred Books. Maha-pagâpati, Gautama's aunt, thrice made to him the request : " It would be well, Lord, if women should be allowed to renounce their homes, and enter the homeless state, under the doctrine and discipline of the Tathâgata." He replied : "Enough, O Gotamî ! let it not please thee that women should be allowed so to do."   Then Mahâ-pagâpati the Gotamî, sad and sorrowful for that the

Blessed One would not permit women to enter the homeless state . . . departed thence weeping and in tears.
And the venerable Ânanda saw her, and said : "Why
standest thou there with swollen feet and covered with
dust, sad and sorrowful, weeping and in tears?" She
tells him, and he thrice makes the request before
Gautama yields. In doing so, he laid down eight chief
Rules for the Bhikkhunîs or female Mendicants. The
following extracts serve to illustrate their subordinate
position : "A Bhikkhunî, even if of a hundred years'
standing, shall make salutation to, shall rise up in the
presence of, shall bow down before, and shall peform all
proper duty towards, a Bhikkhu, if only just initiated.
This is a Rule to be revered and reverenced, honoured
and observed, and her life long never to be transgressed.
. . . When a Bhikkhunî, as novice has been trained
for two years in the Six Rules, she is to ask leave for the
upasampadâ initiation from both Sa*m*ghas (as well that
of Bhikkhus as that of Bhikkhunîs). . . . From
henceforth official admonition by Bhikkhunîs of Bhikkhus
is forbidden, whereas the official admonition of Bhikkhunîs by Bhikkhus is not forbidden."

Gautama told Ânanda that since women had been
admitted, the good law would last only five hundred,
instead of one thousand years ; he added : " Just,
Ânanda, as houses in which there are many women and
but few men are easily violated by robber burglars ; just
so, Ânanda, under whatever doctrine and discipline
women are allowed to go out from the household life into
the homeless state, that religion will not last long. And
just, Ânanda, as when the disease called mildew falls
upon a field of rice in fine condition, that field of rice
does not last long ; just so, Ânanda, under whatsoever
doctrine and discipline women are allowed to go forth
from the household life into the homeless state, that

religion will not last long. And just, Ananda, as when the disease called blight falls upon a field of sugar-cane in good condition, that field of sugar-cane does not continue long ; just so, Ânanda, under whatsoever doctrine or discipline women are allowed to go forth from the household life into the homeless state, that religion does not last long. And just, Ânanda, as a man would in anticipation build an embankment to a great reservoir, beyond which the water should not overpass ; just even so, Ânanda, have I in anticipation laid down these Eight Chief Rules for the Bhikkhunîs, their life long not to be over-passed " (*K*ullavagga, XI., 1-6, *S. B. E.*, vol. xx., p. 320).

It may be urged that Gautama should scarcely be held responsible for adopting these regulations ; that the Eastern mind was so impressed with the idea of the subordination of women that it came to be regarded as a matter of course. The Laws of Manu, for example, enact in regard to women : " In childhood let her be subjected to the will of her father ; in adult life to the will of the man who has led her home ; to her son's will when her husband has died ; a woman is not permitted to enjoy independence " (quoted by Oldenburg, Buddha, p. 377). And yet Easterns could rise to a recognition of woman's true place and worth. There is a passage in the Mahā-bhārata, upon which no Western, even in the nineteenth century, could improve :—

> "A wife is half the man, his truest friend,
> A loving wife is a perpetual spring
> Of virtue, pleasure, wealth ; a faithful wife
> Is his best aid in seeking heavenly bliss ;
> A sweetly-speaking wife is a companion
> In solitude ; a father in advice ;
> A mother in all seasons of distress ;
> A rest in passing through life's wilderness."

(Quoted by Sir Monier-Williams in *The Holy Bible and the Sacred Books of the East*, p. 57).

APPENDIX V.
BUDDHISM AND SUICIDE.

NOTWITHSTANDING the cautions laid down in regard to self-destruction, we find Buddhists, in later times, adopting this course as a speedy mode of deliverance from the sorrows of life. Thus, for example, in "The travels of Fa-hian" (*circ.* A.D. 400) the following story is told :—"Some time ago there was a Bhikshu who walked forwards and backwards, meditating on the impermanency, the sorrow, and vanity of his body. Thus realizing the character of impurity, loathing himself, he drew his knife and would have killed himself. But then he reflected that the Lord of the world had forbidden self-murder. But then again he thought, 'Although this is so, yet I am simply anxious to destroy the three poisonous thieves (evil desire, hatred, and ignorance). Then again he drew the knife and cut his throat. On the first gash, he obtained the degree of Srôtâpanna ; when he had half done the work, he arrived at the condition of Anâgâmin, and after completing the deed, he obtained the position of an Arhat, and entered Nirvâna" (Beal, *Buddhist Records of the Western World*).

In "A Buddhist Catechism," by Subhádra Bhikshu, a different standpoint is urged (p. 51).

"*Q*. Is it wrong to commit suicide ?

"*A*. No ; so long as no wrong is done any one thereby. For man is perfect master of his own life. This needs no proof. But suicide is a very foolish act, for it violently cuts a thread of life which, according to the law of Karma, has to be taken up immediately, and under still less favourable conditions than those which the deluded man tried to escape by it."

There are two passages from the Sacred Books which bear upon the question of suicide ; the first is from the Pârâgika Rules of the Pâtimokkha, "Whatsoever Bhikkhu shall knowingly deprive of life a human being, or shall seek out an assassin against a human being, or shall utter the praises of death, or incite another to self-destruction, saying, 'Ho ! my friend ! what good do you get from this sinful, wretched life ?

death is better to thee than life!'—if, so thinking, and with such an aim, he, by various argument, utter the praises of death or incite another to self-destruction— he, too, is fallen into defeat, he is no longer in com- munion" (*S. B. E.*, vol. xiii., p. 4).

The Second passage is from "The Questions of King Milinda : "Venerable Nâgasena, it has been said by the Blessed One, 'A brother is not, O Bhikkhus, to commit suicide. Whosoever does so, shall be dealt with accord- ing to the law.' And, on the other hand, you (members of the Order), say, 'On whatsoever subject the Blessed One was addressing the disciples, he always, and with various similes, preached to them in order to bring about the destruction of birth, of old age, of disease, and of death. And whosoever overcame birth, old age, disease, and death, him did he honour with the highest praise.' Now if the Blessed One forbade suicide, that saying of yours must be wrong ; but if not, then the prohibition of suicide must be wrong. This too is a double-edged problem now put to you, and you have to solve it."

"The regulation you quote, O king, was laid down by the Blessed One ; and yet is our saying you refer to true. And there is a reason for this, a reason for which the Blessed One both prohibited (the destruction of life), and also (in another sense) instigated us to it.

"What, Nâgasena, may that reason be ?"

"The good man, O king, perfect in uprightness, is like a medicine to men in being an antidote to the poison of evil ; he is like water to men in laying the dust and the impurities of evil dispositions ; he is like a jewel treasure to men in bestowing upon them all attainments in righteousness ; he is like a boat to men, inasmuch as he conveys them to the further shore of the four flooded streams (of lust, individuality, delusion, and ignorance) ; he is like a caravan owner to men, in that he brings them beyond the sandy desert of rebirths ; he is like a mighty rain-cloud to men, in that he fills their hearts with satisfaction ; he is like a teacher to men, in that he trains them in all good ; he is like a good guide to men, in that he points out to them the path of peace. It was in order that so good a man as that—one whose good qualities are so many, so various, so immeasurable— in order that so great a treasure mine of good things—

so full of benefit to all beings—might not be done away
with, that the Blessed One, O king, out of his mercy
towards all beings, laid down this injunction, when he
said, 'A brother is not, O Bhikkhus, to commit suicide.
Whosoever does so, shall be dealt with according to the
law.' This is the reason for which the Blessed One
prohibited (self-slaughter)." (*S. B. E.*, vol. xxxv., p. 273).

APPENDIX VI.
THE CHRISTIAN AND BUDDHIST CANON.

IN the Preface to his translation of "The Questions of
King Milinda," Prof. Rhys Davids has some remarks on
this subject. He writes : "As is well known, Asoka, in
the only one of his edicts, addressed specially to the
members of the Buddhist Order of Mendicants, selects
seven portions of the Buddhist Scriptures, which he
mentions by name, and expresses his desire that not only
the brethren and sisters of the Order, but also the laity,
should constantly learn by heart and reflect upon those
seven. Now not one of the seven titles which occur in
the edict is identical with any of the twenty-nine in the
last list [*i.e.*, a list of the books in the Pâli Pi*t*akas].
Whereupon certain Indianists have rejoiced at being able
to score a point, as they think, against these unbrah-
manical Buddhists, and have jumped to the conclusion
that the Buddhist Canon must be late and spurious ; and
that the Buddhism of Asoka's time must have been very
different from the Buddhism of the Pâli Pi*t*akas. That
would be much the same as if a Japanese scholar, at a
time when he knew little or nothing of Christianity,
except the names of the Books in the Bible, were to have
found an open letter of Constantine's, in which he urges
both the clergy and laity to look upon the Word of God
as their only authority, and to constantly and earnestly
meditate upon the Psalm of the Shepherd, the Words of
Lemuel, the Prophecy of the Servant of the Lord, the
Sermon on the Mount, the Exaltation of Charity, the
Question of Nicodemus, and the Story of the Prodigal
Son—and that our Oriental critic should jump to the
conclusion that the Canonical Books of the Christians

could not have been known in the time of Constantine,
and that the Christianity of Constantine was really
quite different from, and much more simple than, the
Christianity of the Bible.   As a matter of fact, the
existence of such a letter would prove very little, either
way, as to the date of the books in the Bible, as we now
have them.   If our Japanese scholar were to discover
afterwards a Christian work—even much later than the
time of Constantine—in which the Canonical Books of
the Christians were both quoted and referred to, he
would have much surer ground for a sounder historical
criticism.   And he would possibly come to see that the
seven portions selected for special honour and com-
mendation were not intended as an exhaustive list even
of remarkable passages, much less for an exhaustive list
of Canonical Books, but that the number seven was
merely chosen in deference to the sacred character
attaching to that number in the sacred literature.   Such
a book is our Milinda" (*Sacred Books of the East*,
vol. xxxv., p. xxxvii.).

There is undoubtedly force in this reasoning.   But
there could be no stronger statement in proof of the
different footing on which the Christian Canon stands
as contrasted with that of the Buddhists.   We can best
see this by supposing for a moment that what Prof.
Rhys Davids suggests was really the case, namely, that
as authorities for the Canon of the New Testament
we had only a letter of Constantine's, referring to some
few scattered fragments of the Books, and a treatise
by St. Augustine, in which most of the New Testament
Books were mentioned and quoted.   What would the
opponents of Christianity say of such a foundation
for belief in the authenticity and genuineness of our
Sacred Books?   Let any one read the controversies
of the last fifty or sixty years on the New Testament
Canon, since Strauss first published his "*Life of Jesus*";
let any one read the methods of argument adopted
by the Tübingen school of critics, and the desperate
efforts made to overthrow the reliability of our Books
as records of primitive Christianity, and then suppose
that instead of the mass of evidence that can be brought
forward in their favour, we had only the two authorities which Rhys Davids suggests, dating three or four

centuries after the Christian Faith had been founded, and he can readily draw the conclusion that if the evidence was in reality only such, we should have been plainly told that there was no foundation on which to build, that historical criticism could not accept authorities so few in number and so late in date as furnishing valid testimony. Prof. Rhys Davids' remarks, therefore, leave untouched the position I have maintained in Lecture VI., that there is an utter absence of parallelism in the measure of authority attaching to the Christian and the Buddhist Canon.

APPENDIX VII.
The Logia Kuriaka.

THE theory that the earliest Christian document was a collection of the Discourses of our Lord is founded on a statement of Papias, Bishop of Hierapolis in Phrygia, in the first half of the second century. The statement has been preserved in the Ecclesiastical History of Eusebius. It has been so frequently quoted as a proof that the original documents of Christianity have not come down to us, and that our Gospels only possess a secondary authority, that I think it well to give here what Papias states, and then Dr. Salmon's and Bishop Lightfoot's commentaries on his words.

Papias is giving the testimony of John the Elder concerning the Evangelists : " And this, also, the Elder said : Mark, having become the interpreter of Peter, wrote accurately all that he remembered of the things that were either said or done by Christ ; but, however, not in order. For he neither heard the Lord nor followed Him ; but, subsequently, as I said [attached himself to] Peter, who used to frame his teaching to meet the immediate wants [of his hearers], but not as making a connected narrative of our Lord's discourses."

Here there is a difference of reading between λόγων and λογίων : it is important to notice that if λογίων be the true reading, it is used as a synonym for "*the things said or done*" (τὰ λεχθέντα ἢ πραχθέντα). Then follow the words : " Matthew wrote the oracles (τὰ λόγια) in Hebrew, and each one interpreted them as he could" (Routh's *Reliquiæ Sacræ*, vol. i., p. 13, 14). Renan regards these words as proving that the original Gospel of St. Matthew was merely a collection of the discourses of our Lord; and Oldenburg, in the passage which I have quoted, adopts a similar view. The theory rests upon the supposition that by Logia we are to understand discourses. On this point Dr. Salmon says: "But I wholly disbelieve that the word λόγια in the extract from Papias is rightly translated, 'the speeches of our Lord.' Not to speak of the absurdity of supposing a collection of our Lord's sayings to have been made without any history of the occasions on which they were spoken, λόγια is one word, λόγοι another. Examine for yourselves the four passages in which the former word occurs in the New Testament: Acts vii. 38, 'Moses received the lively oracles to give unto us'; Rom. iii. 2, 'To the Jews were committed the oracles of God'; Heb. v. 12, 'Ye have need that we teach you what be the first principles of the oracles of God'; and lastly, 1 Pet. iv. 11, 'If any one speak, let him speak as the oracles of God.' Now when Paul, for example, says that to the Jews were committed the oracles of God, can we imagine that he confines this epithet to those parts of the Old Testament which contained Divine sayings, and that he excludes those narrative parts from which he has himself so often drawn lessons in his Epistles. . . Thus we find that in the New Testament, λόγια has its classical meaning, 'oracles,' and is applied to the inspired utterances of God in His Holy Scriptures. . . We must recollect also that the title of Papias' own work is λογίων κυριακῶν ἐξήγησις, while it is manifest that the book was not confined to treating of our Lord's discourses. I consider the true conclusion to be, that as we find from Justin, that the Gospels were put on the same level with the Old Testament in the public reading of the Church; so we find from Papias that the name λόγια, the oracles, given to the Old Testament Scriptures, was also given to the Gospels, which were called τά κυριακὰ λόγια, the oracles of our Lord. The title of Papias' own work I take as meaning simply 'an exposition of the *Gospels*'; and his statement about Matthew I take as meaning: 'Matthew composed his *Gospel in* Hebrew,' the word

λόγια implying its Scriptural authority. I do not know
any passage where λόγια means discourses ; and I believe the notion that Matthew's Gospel was originally
only a collection of speeches to be a mere dream"
(*Introduction to the New Testament*, p. 117-119).

Similarly Bishop Lightfoot has argued, "We are ex-
pressly told that the Scriptures recognized by Ephraem,
Patriarch of Antioch (about A.D. 525-545), consisted of
'the Old Testament, and the Oracles of the Lord
(τὰ κυριακὰ λόγια), and the Preachings of the Apostles.'
Here we have the very same expression, which occurs in
Papias, and it is obviously employed as a synonyme for
the Gospels. . . [Philo] in one place speaks of the
words in Deut. x. 9, 'The Lord God is His inheritance,'
as an 'oracle' (λόγιον); in another place he quotes as
an 'oracle' (λόγιον), the *narrative* in Genesis iv. 15,
'The Lord God set a mark upon Cain.' Similarly
Clement of Rome writes, 'Ye know well the Sacred
Scriptures, and have studied the Oracles of God'; and
immediately he recalls to their minds the account in
Deut. ix. 12 *seq.* and Exod. xxxii. 7 *seq.*, of which the
point is not any divine precept or prediction, but *the
example of Moses.*"

Bishop Lightfoot adds quotations from Irenæus,
Clement of Alexandria, Origen, and Basil, in proof of
their usage of the word λόγια, as signifying " oracles,"
not "discourses" (*Contemporary Review*, August, 1875,
p. 399).

I have given these extracts, because it seems to be an
important element in the argument that the conception
which the early Christians had of our Lord, differed from
that which the early Buddhists had of Gautama. That
it was, as I have already stated, the Person of Christ
and the Acts of His Life that formed the centre of the
earliest Christian teaching. When such a writer as
Oldenburg argues that it was our Lord's *words* alone
that were at first deemed to be of sufficient importance
to be preserved and perpetuated, it seemed desirable to
point out that the only foundation for such an idea rests
upon an untenable interpretation of what Papias says.

PUBLICATIONS

OF THE

Society for Promoting Christian Knowledge.

WORKS BY THE
REV. F. BOURDILLON, M.A.

				s.	d.
Bedside Readings. Being short portions of Holy Scripture, with a simple Commentary.					
SERIES I. 12mo.			*Cloth boards*	1	4
SERIES II.			ditto	1	4
The two Series in a volume			ditto	2	0
The Week of Mourning; or, SHORT AND SIMPLE EXPOSITIONS OF SCRIPTURE, FOR THE USE OF THE BEREAVED			*Cloth*	0	10
Alone with God; or, HELPS TO THOUGHTS AND PRAYER, FOR THE USE OF THE SICK; BASED ON SHORT PASSAGES OF SCRIPTURE			*Cloth boards*	1	0
Lesser Lights. SERIES I. Post 8vo. ..			*Cloth boards*	2	6
Ditto SERIES II.			ditto	2	6
Straight On; DIRECTIONS, ENCOURAGEMENT, AND WARNINGS ADDRESSED ESPECIALLY TO YOUNG MEN, WHO HAVE SET OUT ON THE WAY OF ETERNAL LIFE ..			*Cloth boards*	1	0
A Quiet Visitor. A Book for Lying-in Women. Post 8vo.			*Cloth boards*	0	10
Our Own Book. Very Plain Reading for People in Humble Life. Post 8vo.			*Cloth boards*	1	0
Volume of Tracts. SERIES I.			*Cloth boards*	1	6
Ditto SERIES II.			*(large type)* *Cloth boards*	1	6

WORKS BY THE AUTHOR OF
"The Chronicles of the SCHÖNBERG-COTTA FAMILY."

	s.	d.
The Beatitudes. Thoughts for All Saints' Day. Post 8vo. .. .. *Cloth boards*	1	6
"By the Mystery of Thy Holy Incarnation." Post 8vo. *Cloth boards*	1	6
"By Thy Cross and Passion." Thoughts on the words spoken around and on the Cross.. .. *Cloth boards*	1	6
"By Thy Glorious Resurrection and Ascension." Easter Thoughts. Post 8vo. .. .. .. *Cloth boards*	1	6
"By the Coming of the Holy Ghost." Thoughts for Whitsuntide. Post 8vo. .. .. .. *Cloth boards*	1	6
The True Vine. Post 8vo. .. .. .. *Cloth boards*	1	6
The Great Prayer of Christendom. Thoughts on the Lord's Prayer. Post 8vo. .. .. *Cloth boards*	1	6
An Old Story of Bethlehem. One link in the great Pedigree. Fcap. 4to, with six plates, beautifully printed in colours .. .. *Cloth boards*	2	6
Three Martyrs of the Nineteenth Century. Studies from the Lives of Gordon, Livingstone, and Patteson. Crown 8vo. .. .. *Cloth boards*	3	6
Martyrs and Saints of the First Twelve Centuries. Studies from the Lives of the Black-letter Saints of the English Calendar. Crown 8vo. .. *Cloth boards*	5	0
Against the Stream. The Story of an Heroic Age in England. With eight page woodcuts. Crown 8vo. *Cloth boards*	4	0
Conquering and to Conquer. A Story of Rome in the days of St. Jerome. With four page woodcuts. Crown 8vo. .. .. *Cloth boards*	2	6
Lapsed not Lost. A Story of Roman Carthage. Crown 8vo. .. .. *Cloth boards*	2	6
Sketches of the Women of Christendom. Crown 8vo. *Cloth boards*	3	6
Thoughts and Characters. Being Selections from the Writings of the Author of "The Schönberg-Cotta Family," &c Crown 8vo. .. .. *C oth boards*	3	6

THE HOME LIBRARY.

A Series of Books illustrative of Church History, &c., specially, but not exclusively, adapted for Sunday Reading.

Crown 8vo, cloth boards, 3s. 6d. each.

Black and White. Mission Stories. By H. A. FORDE.

Charlemagne. By the Rev. E. L. CUTTS, B.A. With Map.

Constantine the Great. The Union of the Church and State By the Rev. E. L. CUTTS, B.A.

Great English Churchmen; or, Famous Names in English Church History and Literature. By W. H. DAVENPORT ADAMS.

John Hus. The Commencement of resistance to Papal Authority on the part of the Inferior Clergy. By the Rev. A. H. WRATISLAW.

Judæa and Her Rulers, from Nebuchadnezzar to Vespasian. By M. BRAMSTON. With Map.

Mazarin. By the late GUSTAVE MASSON.

Military Religious Orders of the Middle Ages; the Hospitallers, the Templars, the Teutonic Knights, and others. By the Rev. F. C. WOODHOUSE, M.A.

Mitslav; or, the Conversion of Pomerania. By the late Right Rev. ROBERT MILMAN, D.D. With Map.

Narcissus: A Tale of Early Christian Times. By the Right Rev. W. BOYD CARPENTER, Bishop of Ripon.

Richelieu. By the late GUSTAVE MASSON.

Sketches of the Women of Christendom. Dedicated to the Women of India. By the author of "The Chronicles of the Schönberg-Cotta Family."

The Church in Roman Gaul. By the Rev. R. TRAVERS SMITH.

The Churchman's Life of Wesley. By R. DENNY URLIN, Esq.

The House of God the Home of Man. By Rev. Canon JELF.

The Inner Life, as Revealed in the Correspondence of Celebrated Christians. Edited by the late Rev. T. ERSKINE.

The Life of the Soul in the World; its Nature, Needs, Dangers, Sorrows, Aids, and Joys. By the Rev. F. C. WOODHOUSE, M.A.

The North-African Church. By Rev. JULIUS LLOYD. With Map

Thoughts and Characters: being Selections from the Writings of the author of the "Schönberg-Cotta Family."

THE
DAWN OF EUROPEAN LITERATURE.

A set of Works designed to present the chief races of Europe as they emerge out of pre-historic darkness into the light furnished by their earliest recorded words.

Post 8vo., cloth boards, 2s. 6d. each.

Anglo-Saxon Literature. By the Rev. Professor EARLE.

French Literature. By the late GUSTAVE MASSON, B.A.

Slavonic Literature. By W. R. MORFILL, M.A.

THE
FATHERS FOR ENGLISH READERS.

A Series of Monograms on the Chief Fathers of the Church, the Fathers Selected being centres of influence at important periods of Church History, and in important spheres of action.

Fcap. 8vo., cloth boards, 2s. each.

Leo the Great. By the Rev. CHARLES GORE, M.A.

Gregory the Great. By the Rev. J. BARMBY, B.D.

Saint Ambrose : his Life, Times, and Teaching. By the Rev. ROBINSON THORNTON, D.D.

Saint Athanasius : his Life and Times. By the Rev. R. WHELER BUSH. (2s. 6d.)

Saint Augustine. By the Rev. E. L. CUTTS, B.A.

Saint Basil the Great. By the Rev. R. T. SMITH, B.D.

Saint Bernard : Abbot of Clairvaux, A.D. 1091—1153. By the Rev. S. J. EALES, D.C.L. (2s. 6d.)

Saint Jerome. By the Rev. EDWARD L. CUTTS, B.A.

Saint Hilary of Poitiers, and Saint Martin of Tours. By the Rev. J. GIBSON CAZENOVE, D.D.

Saint John of Damascus. By the Rev. J. H. LUPTON.

Saint Patrick : his Life and Teaching. By the Rev. E. J. NEWELL, M.A. (2s. 6d.)

Synesius of Cyrene, Philosopher and Bishop. By ALICE GARDNER.

The Apostolic Fathers. By the Rev. H. S. HOLLAND.

The Defenders of the Faith ; or, The Christian Apologists of the Second and Third Centuries. By the Rev. F. WATSON, M.A.

The Venerable Bede. By the Rev. G. F. BROWNE.

PUBLICATIONS OF THE SOCIETY.

ANCIENT HISTORY FROM THE MONUMENTS.

This Series of Books is chiefly intended to illustrate the Sacred Scriptures by the results of recent Monumental Researches in the East.

Fcap. 8vo., cloth boards, 2s. each.

Assyria, from the Earliest Times to the Fall of Nineveh. By the late GEORGE SMITH, of the British Museum.

Sinai: from the Fourth Egyptian Dynasty to the Present Day. By the late HENRY S. PALMER, Major R.E., F.R.A.S. With Map.

Babylonia (The History of). By the late GEORGE SMITH. Edited by the Rev. A. H. SAYCE.

Greek Cities and Islands of Asia Minor. By the late W. S. W. VAUX, M.A.

Egypt from the Earliest Times to B.C. 300. By the late S. BIRCH, LL.D.

Persia from the Earliest Period to the Arab Conquest. By the late W. S. W. VAUX, M.A.

NON-CHRISTIAN RELIGIOUS SYSTEMS.

A Series of Manuals which furnish in a brief and popular form an accurate account of the great Non-Christian Religious Systems of the World.

Fcap. 8vo., cloth boards, 2s. 6d. each.

Buddhism—Being a Sketch of the Life and Teachings of Gautama, the Buddha. By T. W. RHYS DAVIDS. With Map.

Buddhism in China. By the Rev. S. BEAL. With Map.

Confucianism and Taouism. By Professor ROBERT K. DOUGLAS, of the British Museum. With Map.

Hinduism. By Professor MONIER WILLIAMS. With Map.

Islam and its Founder. By J. W. H. STOBART. With Map.

Islam as a Missionary Religion. By CHARLES R. HAINES. (2s

The Coran—Its Composition and Teaching, and the Testimony it bears to the Holy Scriptures. By Sir WILLIAM MUIR, K.C.S.I.

CHIEF ANCIENT PHILOSOPHIES.

This Series of Books deals with the chief systems of Ancient Thought, not merely as dry matters of History, but as having a bearing on Modern Speculation.

Fcap. 8vo., cloth boards, 2s. 6d. each.

Epicureanism. By WILLIAM WALLACE, Esq., Fellow and Tutor of Merton College, Oxford.

Stoicism. By Rev. W. W. CAPES, Fellow of Hertford College.

Aristotelianism. The Ethics of Aristotle. By the Rev. J. GREGORY SMITH, M.A., Hon. LL.D. The Logical Treatises, the Metaphysics, the Psychology, the Politics. By the Rev. W. GRUNDY, M.A.

DIOCESAN HISTORIES.

This series furnishes a perfect Library of English Ecclesiastical History. Each volume is complete in itself, and the possibility of repetition has been carefully guarded against.

Fcap. 8vo., with Map, cloth boards.

Bath and Wells. By the Rev. W. HUNT. 2s. 6d.

Canterbury. By the Rev. R. C. JENKINS. 3s. 6d.

Carlisle. By RICHARD S. FERGUSON, ESQ. 2s. 6d.

Chichester. By the Rev. W. R. W. STEPHENS. With Map and Plan. 2s. 6d.

Durham. By the Rev. J. L. LOW. With Map and Plan. 2s. 6d.

Hereford. By the Rev. Canon PHILLOTT. 3s.

Lichfield. By the Rev. W. BERESFORD. 2s. 6d.

Norwich. By the Rev. A. JESSOP, D.D. 2s. 6d.

Oxford. By the Rev. E. MARSHALL. 2s. 6d.

Peterborough. By the Rev. G. A. POOLE, M.A. 2s. 6d.

Salisbury. By the Rev. W. H. JONES. With Map and Plan. 2s. 6d.

St. Asaph. By the Ven. Archdeacon THOMAS. 2s. 6d.

St. David's. By the Rev. Canon BEVAN. With Map. 2s. 6d.

Winchester. By the Rev. W. BENHAM, B.D. 3s.

Worcester. By the Rev. J. GREGORY SMITH, M.A., and the Rev. PHIPPS ONSLOW, M.A. 3s. 6d.

York. By the Rev. Canon ORNSBY, M.A., F.S.A. 3s. 6d.

EARLY BRITAIN.

This Series of Books has for its aim the presentation of Early Britain at great historic periods. Each volume is the work of an accredited specialist, and the whole gives the result of the most recent critical examinations of our Early Records.

Fcap. 8vo, cloth boards.

	s.	d.
Anglo-Saxon Britain. By GRANT ALLEN, B.A. With Map	2	6
Celtic Britain. By Professor RHYS. With two Maps ..	3	0
Norman Britain, By the Rev. W. HUNT. With Map..	2	0
Post-Norman Britain. By HENRY G. HEWLETT. With Map	3	0
Roman Britain. By Rev. Prebendary SCARTH. With Map	2	6

CHURCH HYMNS.

Nos. 1 to 7, in Various Sizes and Bindings, ranging in price from 1d. to 4s. 8d.

Church Hymns, with Tunes. Edited by Sir ARTHUR SULLIVAN. Crown 8vo, Fcap. 4to, and Folio (Organ copy) in various Bindings, from 2s. to £1 1s.

Common Prayer Book and Church Hymns. Bound in One Volume, and in Two Volumes in Cases. Can be had in various Sizes and Bindings, from 5d. to 4s.

Common Prayer Book and Church Hymns, with Tunes. Brevier, 8vo, Limp paste grain roan, red edges, 6s.

COMMENTARY ON THE BIBLE.

Crown 8vo., cloth boards, red edges, 4s. ; half calf, 10s. ; whole calf, 12s. each volume.

Old Testament. By Various Authors.

Vol. I., containing the Pentateuch. With Maps and Plans.

Vol. II., containing the Historical Books, Joshua to Esther. With Maps and Plans.

Vol. III., containing the Poetical Books, Job to Song of Solomon.

Old Testament :—

    Vol. IV., containing the Prophetical Books, Isaiah to Malachi. With two Maps.

    Vol. V., containing the Apocryphal Books.

New Testament :—

    Vol. I., containing the Four Gospels. By the Right Rev. W. WALSHAM How, Bishop of Wakefield. With Maps and Plans.

    Vol. II., containing the Acts, Epistles, and Revelation. By Various Authors. With Map.

THE ROMANCE OF SCIENCE.

A series of books which will show that science has for the masses as great interest and more edification than the romances of the day.

Small Post 8vo, cloth boards.

The Birth and Growth of Worlds. A Lecture by Professor A. H. GREEN, M.A., F.R.S. 1s.

Soap-Bubbles, and the Forces which Mould Them. Being a course of Three Lectures delivered at the London Institution in December, 1889, and January, 1890, before a juvenile audience. By C. V. BOYS, A.R.S.M., F.R.S. With numerous diagrams. 2s. 6d.

Spinning Tops. The Operatives' Lecture of the British Association Meeting at Leeds, September, 1890. By Professor J. PERRY, M.E., D.Sc., F.R.S. With numerous diagrams. 2s. 6d.

Diseases of Plants. By Professor MARSHALL WARD. With Numerous Illustrations. 2s. 6d.

The Story of a Tinder-Box. A course of Lectures delivered before a Juvenile Auditory at the London Institution. By CHARLES MEYMOTT TIDY, M.B., M.S., F.C.S. With numerous Illustrations. 2s.

Time and Tide. A Romance of the Moon. By Sir ROBERT S. BALL, LL.D., Royal Astronomer of Ireland. With Illustrations. 2s. 6d.

LONDON:

NORTHUMBERLAND AVENUE, CHARING CROSS, W.C.

43, QUEEN VICTORIA STREET, E.C.

BRIGHTON : 135, NORTH STREET.